Real Life Reading and Writing at Work

edited by Jim McNicholas
Senior Lecturer,
Edge Hill College of Higher Education

Careers Consultant: Rob Ward
Edge Hill College of Higher Education

Heinemann Educational Books
London

Heinemann Educational Books Ltd
22 Bedford Square, London WC1B 3HH
LONDON   EDINBURGH   MELBOURNE   AUCKLAND
HONG KONG   SINGAPORE   KUALA LUMPUR   NEW DELHI
IBADAN   NAIROBI   JOHANNESBURG
PORTSMOUTH (NH)   KINGSTON   PORT OF SPAIN

© First published 1985

British Library Cataloguing in Publication Data

Real life reading and writing at work.

I. McNicholas, Jim
808'.042'076   LB1050

ISBN 0-435-10525-6

Printed and bound in Great Britain by
Thomson Litho Ltd, East Kilbride, Scotland
Phototypesetting by Georgia Ltd, Liverpool

Acknowledgements

The authors would like to thank the following for permission to reproduce copyright material:
British Telecom for extracts from Yellow Pages. 'Yellow Pages' is a registered trade mark of British Telecommunications plc in the United Kingdom; the Controller of Her Majesty's Stationery Office for sections from form P15 Coding Claim (Crown copyright) and from DHSS leaflet SB.1 November 1983 edition (Crown copyright).

Contents

Introduction

UNIT 1	*Life after school*	*1*
	Youth Training Scheme	2
	What I need to know about jobs and training scheme places	4
	Interests, abilities and characteristics	6
	The job jargon	8
	Benefits and responsibilities	10
	Revision	13
UNIT 2	*Job hunting*	*15*
	Help with job hunting (or getting a YTS place)	16
	Applying for the Youth Training Scheme (YTS)	18
	Situations vacant ads	20
	Answering ads	22
	Making the first move	25
	Application forms	28
	The interview	30
	Leaving school and after	32
	Revision	34
UNIT 3	*Office jobs*	*37*
	Clerk	38
	Receptionist/telephonist	40
	Office machine operator	42
	Typist	44
	Secretary	46
	Revision	48
UNIT 4	*Social jobs*	*51*
	Shop assistant	52
	Dry-cleaners shop assistant	54
	Waiter/waitress	56
	Nurse (E.N. (G))	58
	Cashier (in a shop)	60
	Revision	62
UNIT 5	*Practical jobs*	*65*
	Assembly worker	66
	Carpenter	68
	Plumber	70
	Electrician	72
	Motor mechanic	74
	Revision	76
UNIT 6	*Active/outdoor jobs*	*79*
	Forecourt sales staff	80
	Delivery person	82
	Building worker	84
	Glazier	86
	General farm worker	88
	Revision	90

UNIT 7	*Artistic jobs*	93
	Hairdresser	94
	Florist's assistant	96
	Photographer	98
	Dressmaker	100
	Signwriter	102
	Revision	104
UNIT 8	*Public service jobs*	107
	Postman/postwoman	108
	Police officer	110
	Fireman/firewoman	112
	Armed services	114
	Community Service Volunteers	116
	Revision	118
	More about the jobs in this book	121
	Personal notes	122

Introduction

Most of us want to get a job when we leave school. We may get a part-time job or other work experience while at school. We may take a training course after we leave. Whatever we do, reading and writing skills are necessary. They are needed in every job from shop assistant to company manager. They are needed when we apply for a job or course. You even need them if you are out of work, for claiming benefits for instance.

The reading and writing skills covered in this book are shown in real-life situations. The skills, though, do not apply only to one special job. For example, the map-reading skills included in 'Delivery person' (page 82) may be important to others. Coach drivers, postal workers and doctors need these skills. And most people would find them useful.

How to use this book

Real Life Reading and Writing at Work is divided into units. Each unit contains a group of topics which are related to each other. Each topic (usually a two-page section) deals with reading and writing skills in a lifelike situation. The first two units are more general. They deal with life after school and looking for work.

* Skim through the Contents list. This will give you an idea of the jobs covered.
* Choose any topic and open the book at that page. Most topics include:

   Introduction – a short explanation of the way in which the skills relate to the job;
   Words you need – new words introduced and explained;
   Information – notes and pictures about the topic;
   Questions and exercises – activities needing answers based on the information provided.
Some topics include:
   Tips – hints to help you develop your skills.

There is a revision section at the end of each unit. It tests the skills learned in that unit. You can measure your own personal progress in this way.

Real Life Reading and Writing at Work starts you thinking about jobs. Practise the reading and writing skills needed. They can help you whether you are in or out of work.

Unit 1 Life after school

Times are changing!

In the past school-leavers often went directly into jobs. Now many will enter training schemes either as employees or trainees. This change has come about because of the Youth Training Scheme (YTS). YTS is one of many things you should know about life after school. Most people still hope to find work one day; and YTS aims to help us learn working skills. Therefore it is still important for us to think about 'jobs'. Also we should think about the training places that are available.

This unit centres on the reading and writing skills needed in work or training. It is also about your interests and abilities. How best can you use those qualities? Practise these skills before you go hunting for jobs or places on a training scheme.

Youth Training Scheme 2
Some basic information

What I need to know about jobs and training scheme places 4
Thinking about jobs and schemes

Interests, abilities and characteristics 6
Which jobs and schemes suit us

The job jargon 8
The new words to be learned

Benefits and responsibilities 10
Your rights and duties

Revision 13

Youth Training Scheme

You may have heard about the Youth Training Scheme (YTS). Perhaps you have seen adverts for YTS on television. The scheme offers training and work experience for all under 18 who have no job or place at college. This should help them find their feet and learn some job skills. The scheme is run by the Manpower Services Commission (MSC) and mostly funded by the Government. These pages will help you understand about YTS. Your Careers Officer should be able to tell you more about YTS. It could be useful to know what benefits and opportunities it offers.

*Read the **Words you need**. Study the information on YTS. Then answer the questions.

Words you need

allowance type of pay; money to meet expenses
careers officer person whose job is to advise you on your career
community project scheme to help local groups, e.g. playgroups
employed person who has a job
employer person who employs you
employee person who works for someone else
permanent lasting; long-term
trainee person on a training scheme
unemployed person who has no job

Information on YTS

YTS is organized in two ways: 'A' Schemes and 'B' Schemes.

A Schemes are mostly based with employers. These are for employed and unemployed young people. Employed young people will be paid a wage. The young unemployed (called *trainees*) will get a training allowance. Most young people in A Schemes will probably be unemployed.

B Schemes are based in training workshops, community projects or based in colleges. These are only for unemployed young people. They will be paid a training allowance.

There are many more A Schemes than B Schemes. If you finish the scheme you may have no permanent job to go to. (For information on what to do then see page 32.)

The benefits of YTS to a trainee	Allowance of £26.25 per week; no tax to pay; no National Insurance contributions to pay; entitled to 18 days paid holiday plus Bank Holidays;
and... most importantly	some skills useful in later adult and working life; some experience of working life; a certificate to show what you can do at the end of the scheme.

Are there any **disadvantages**? Well, there are drawbacks.

These may apply to you especially if you are a trainee	You have to pay the first £4 of travelling expenses out of your £26.25 allowance; there may not be a scheme in your area that suits you; there is no guarantee of a permanent job at the end (though you may have more chance in schemes based with employers).

? Questions

1. Who runs YTS? _____

2. If a trainee, how much of an allowance will you get?

3. How can you learn more about local YTS schemes? _____

4. Suppose you are working in a YTS place as a trainee. Your weekly fares come to £3.50. Can you claim this from your employer?

5. If a trainee, would you pay tax or National Insurance from your allowance? _____

6. Who are YTS A Schemes mostly based with? _____

7. Could you be employed and on a YTS B Scheme? _____

8. If an employee in YTS, will you get more or less than £26.25 a week?

9. Fill in the words in the blanks below:
   a. An _____ is a person you work for.
   b. An _____ person has no job.
   c. An _____ works for a boss.
   d. An _____ person has a job.

10. If a trainee, how much paid holiday should you get?

11. Think of the benefits of YTS. Which do you think would be the most important for you?

    Why? _____

12. Write down here the other benefits of YTS: _____

13. What is the most serious disadvantage of YTS in your view?

14. Why? _____

15. What other disadvantages are there? _____

16. If you are a trainee, would you prefer a scheme based
    a. with an employer? _____
    b. in a college? _____
    c. with a community project? _____
    d. in a training workshop? _____
    Why? _____

17. Discuss some types of YTS project with a friend.
    Name some projects you'd like to know more about.

What I need to know about jobs and training scheme places

Jobs are like people: each one is a bit different from the next. So how can we tell which sorts of jobs we might like? The exercises in this section offer some ways of helping us think about jobs. They could also apply to training scheme places.

*Read the **Words you need** carefully. Then study the sections that follow, answering the questions as you go.

Words you need

employer person who employs you
category class, group or division
creative having ability to create, to make something original
irregular not normal
manual mainly using the hands

prospects reasonable hopes
provided given; supplied
punctual on time; prompt
respected well thought of
social relating to society; meeting people and getting on with them

Job families

Because some jobs are similar to each other, they can be grouped together. We call these groups 'job families'. For example, the following jobs can be grouped together because they are indoor jobs:

> warehouse worker   sales assistant   hairdresser

Put down three jobs for each of the following job families:

Job family	Jobs
Outdoor jobs	_____
Practical jobs	_____
Office jobs	_____

How many other job families can you think of?_____

YTS uses a special system of job families. Ask your Careers Officer about these.

Jobs chart

Different jobs may belong to different job families but, like members of families, they are individuals too. We can also think about what individual jobs are like. Look at the chart below (✓ Yes, X No, ? Unsure).

Job	Indoor	Good prospects	Need GCSEs	Get up early	Manual	Clothes provided	Meet people
a. Farm worker	X	?	X	✓	✓	?	X
b. Hairdresser	✓	?	X	X	✓	✓	✓
c. Nurse	✓	?	✓	✓	✓	✓	✓
d. Sales							
e. Teacher							
f. Typist							
g.							
h.							
i.							

Complete the chart for categories d, e and f. Add three more jobs that interest you at g, h and i. Put X, ✓ or ? for each one. You may be unsure about some. For instance, we have put ? for a farmer's prospects. A farmer could work on a big farm and become a supervisor in time. He or she might be able to save and buy a small farm, or always remain a farmworker.

Good points and bad points

Most jobs have good and bad points. Think of an air hostess, for instance. We might agree on these good and bad points:

Job	Good points	Bad points
Air hostess	Travel; see the world; good pay; meet interesting people; smart uniform provided.	Irregular hours; tiring work (on your feet a lot); needs lots of patience; no settled home life.

Now fill in what you see as the good and bad points for these jobs:

Gardener _____ _____

Shop assistant _____ _____

? Questions

1 Write down two jobs from the jobs chart that need GCSEs. _____

2 Workers may lose pay if they are not punctual. Can you think of other good reasons for being punctual? _____

3 Which jobs in the jobs chart would you like to know more about? _____

4 Nurses get up early and work irregular hours. What effects must this have on their social life? _____

5 Write down two jobs that are well respected. Why do you think people respect these jobs? _____

6 Pick one job from those you have added to the Jobs chart. Write in its good and bad points here:

Job	Good points	Bad points

Interests, abilities and characteristics

Many different jobs may interest you. Do they suit your *interests, abilities* and *characteristics*? It is important to know if they do. Remember – abilities are not something gained only at school. We may not be fitted for certain jobs at present. But we can learn! We can develop our skills and abilities throughout the whole of life.

* Read the **Words you need**. Can you remember their meanings? Study the information on interests, abilities and characteristics. Then answer the questions.

Words you need

ability being able to do something
characteristics personal qualities; what makes you *you*
classification group or class
interests things you like doing

journalist person who writes for newspapers or magazines
literate good at reading and writing
numerate good at numbers
persuading winning people over; convincing

Interests

Everyone can have different types of interests and abilities. Look at this classification of interests:

Scientific – interested in knowing how and why things work;
General service – interested in providing people with a service;
Social service – interested in helping people with problems;
Persuading/influencing – interested in organizing or dealing with people;
Literary – interested in using words;
Artistic – interested in artistic things;
Computational – interested in working with numbers;
Practical – interested in working with one's hands;
Nature – interested in working with plants and animals;
Outside/active – interested in being outdoors and active.

? Questions

1 Write down the classification that these jobs best fit into:
a Computer operator _____
b Travelling sales representative _____
c Zoo keeper _____
d Journalist _____
e Hairdresser _____
f Bricklayer _____
2 Write down three of your interests. Put down the classification they fit into best:

Abilities and characteristics

Abilities and characteristics are closely linked. A person may have a natural ability for something because they already have certain characteristics, but it is possible to learn how to do something. Some examples of characteristics and abilities are given here:

Physical characteristics	Learnt abilities	Personal characteristics
Athletic	Creative skills	Careful
Attractive	Drawing skills	Cheerful
Clear voice	Good memory	Friendly
Fit	Handwriting skills	Good listener
Good eyesight	Literate	Good at giving orders
Good hearing	Map-reading skills	Good at taking orders
Nimble	Numerate	Hardworking
Short	Practical (e.g. crafts)	Honest
Strong	Scientific	Punctual
Tall	Typing skills	Tactful

? Questions

3 Different jobs required very different physical abilities. For instance, a jockey is usually _____; a policeman is usually _____.

4 John wants a job in a factory doing electrical assembly work. He will need nimble fingers. Name another physical ability he will need:
_____
_____

5 Patience is a characteristic needed by nurses. Put down three other characteristics they may need:
_____
_____

6 What abilities must apprentice engineers learn? Put down as many as you can think of:
_____
_____

7 A telephone operator needs the following qualities:

                Physical characteristics   *Learnt abilities*   *Personal characteristics*
                Clear voice   Literate   Good listener
                                               Numerate   Cheerful
                                               Good memory Friendly

What qualities might the following jobs require?

Policeman _____

Clerk _____

Door-to-door sales representative _____

8 Write down your interests and abilities:
_____
_____

9 What sorts of jobs can someone with your interests and abilities do? Write them here:
_____

The job jargon

Leaving school and getting a job or training place means many changes. You will have to adjust to longer hours and shorter holidays. On your pay slip you will see the word *deductions*. What does this mean? There is a whole stock of new words to be learned. We have called this the job jargon. Some of this relates to training schemes too. The following exercises will help to make the job jargon clear.

*Read the **Words you need**. Study the information on job jargon. Then answer the questions.

Words you need

contract agreement
deductions money taken away
jargon special words, often confusing

induction introduction to a new job or training scheme
redundant put out of a job; no longer needed

Job jargon

Apprenticeship: an agreement between employer and worker. The employer agrees to train the worker. In return, the worker agrees to stay with the employer for a period of time (usually the length of the training – 3 or 4 years).
Bonus: agreed extra payment, generally for additional work or for overtime.
Clocking on and off: recording the time you start and finish work.
Contract of employment: a document containing the terms under which a worker is employed (e.g. number of hours worked; pay). An agreement between employer and worker.
Day release: spending one day a week at college, becoming qualified for the job you are doing.
Deductions: money taken from your pay, like income tax and National Insurance.
Gross pay: the total amount of pay before deductions.
Induction: introduction to workplace, workmates and conditions.
Laid-off: being stopped from working by an employer (usually because there is not enough work to do).
On-the-job training: being taught how to do a job while working at it.
Overtime: extra hours worked, usually for extra pay.
Piecework: work paid for by the amount of work you actually do.
Redundant: put out of work. After long service you could get a special payment called *redundancy pay*.
Week in hand: working a week before getting paid. This means getting your first week's wages in the second week, and so on.

? Questions

1. Which of these workers might be paid piecework: a teacher, a dressmaker, or a sales assistant? _____

2. The boss gives you extra pay at Christmas. What is this payment called? _____

3. What does 'day release' mean? _____

4. A boy becomes an apprentice joiner at the age of sixteen. How old will he be when his apprenticeship ends? _____

5. Net pay is your pay after deductions. What is pay *before* deductions called? _____

6. If you were 'laid off' for the summer, what would this mean? _____

7. I lose my job. This means I am made:
   a deduction
   b induction
   c redundant?

8. Pay day is Friday. I start working (a five-day week) on Monday 1st August. I work a week in hand. On what date do I get paid? _____

9. When workers enter the factory in the morning they often _____ on.

10. If an employer underpays you, he may be breaking the law. He has broken his agreement with you. What is the proper name for this agreement? _____

11. Name some jobs that provide on-the-job training: _____

12. You may know some YTS jargon. Write it here: _____
    But do you know what it means? _____
    If not, how can you find out? _____

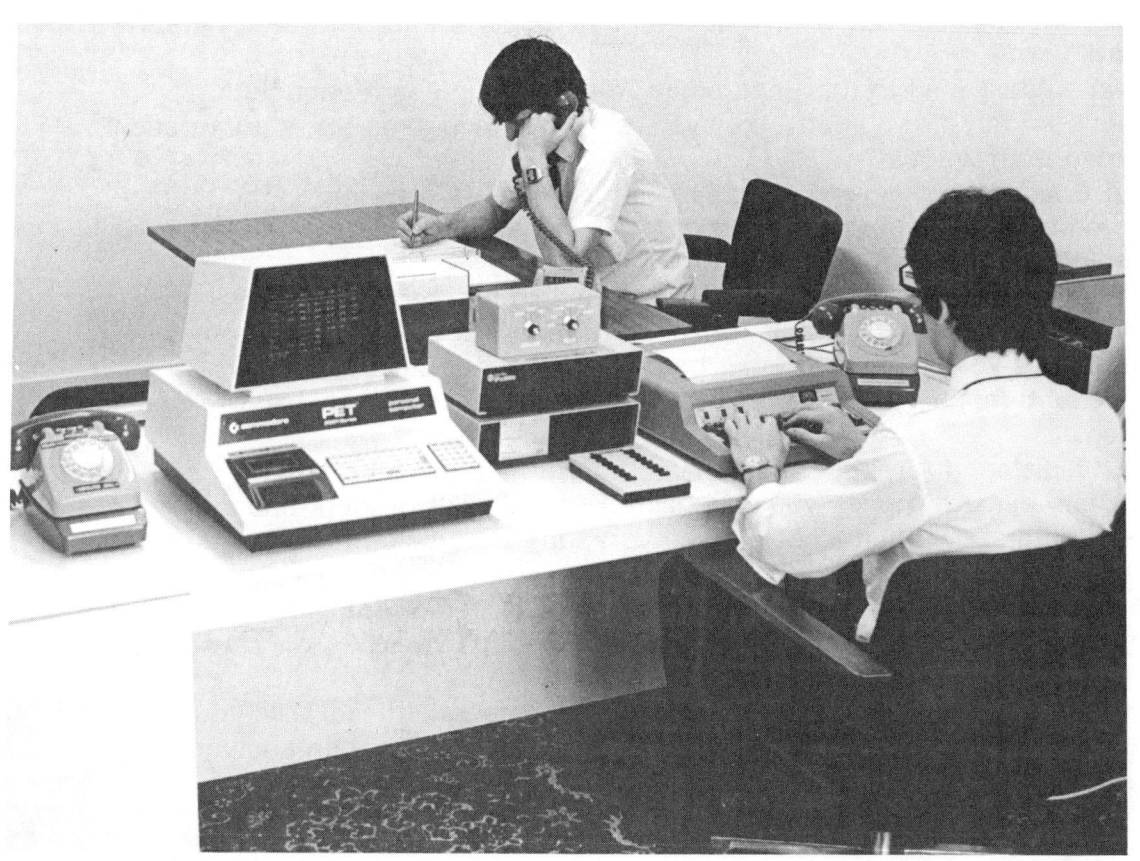

Benefits and responsibilities

We have looked at job jargon. Now we should look at another type of jargon. This is to do with the benefits and responsibilities of being a worker. We should know what these are. If we don't, we may lose out in lots of ways.

The exercises here will help you to understand this jargon. They will help you to discover your rights and your duties. You should then know where and how to make claims. You should also know what you are responsible for.

*Read the **Words you need**. Then read the benefits and responsibilities jargon. Answer the questions.

Words you need

benefits rights; allowances
claimant person who makes a claim
contribute give to a common fund
contributions payments to a fund
deducted taken away
registering signing your name
responsibilities duties; things we are chargeable for
supplementary additional; extra

Benefits and responsibilities jargon

B1: a form for unemployed people to claim supplementary benefit.
DHSS: Department of Health and Social Security (the Government Department that pays supplementary benefit).
DE: Department of Employment (the Government Department that pays unemployment benefit).
Income tax: amount paid to the Government (provided you earn enough).
PAYE: stands for Pay-as-you-earn, the system by which income tax is automatically deducted from wages.
National Insurance: a scheme to which almost all workers contribute. The money collected by the Government is used to pay benefits (e.g. sickness benefit, unemployment benefit).
National Insurance number: a number given to people before they leave school. Everyone's number is different. It is used to record the National Insurance contributions you make (and what benefits you are entitled to).
Sickness benefit: money paid by the DHSS if you cannot work because of illness or accident.
Signing on: registering for work or supplementary/unemployment benefit.
Supplementary benefit: money you can claim if you are out of work and a) have not worked before, or b) have not worked very long. The benefit is often called 'social security'.
Unemployment benefit: money paid to an unemployed person (provided a certain number of National Insurance contributions have been paid).
Benefits
   Leaflet SB1 (obtainable from Post Offices and Careers Offices) tells you about benefits. Read the part of SB1 opposite and the footnote. Then answer the questions.

? Questions

1 You are 17 and have left school. How much benefit are you entitled to?

2 How much more would you get if you were 18?

3 You do not live at home. You live with friends. How much extra should you get?

4 You are a young single person paying rent. How much supplementary benefit are you entitled to?

5 Where can you obtain copies of leaflet SB1?

6 You have a job, part-time, one day a week. From this you earn £10. What should happen to your supplementary benefit?

7 Name two ways in which you may be entitled to more benefit.

8 Name three types of people who can claim supplementary benefit.

9 If you want to know more about benefits, where should you ask?

10 Where does the money come from to pay for benefits?

Footnote
You can claim supplementary benefit if you are: over pension age; too sick or disabled to work; bringing up children on your own; only able to work part-time; looking after a disabled relative.

Responsibilities

When you start work there will be deductions from your wages. Some of these will go to pay income tax – one of your new responsibilities. How will your employer know how much tax to deduct? Well, you will have to complete a form like the one below.

? Questions

1. Study the Coding Claim form shown below. You are a school-leaver. Why would an employer give you this form?
   _____
   _____

2. When completed, where would you send this form?
   _____

3. If you do not send in the form, what may happen?
   _____

4. You have a full-time and a part-time job. Which should you fill in?
   A only ____; B only ____; A and B ____.

5. A second job is taxable. Name two other things mentioned on the form that are taxable.
   _____

6. Fill in the form below. Pretend you are a salesperson at Boots the Chemists. You also have a part-time job at a petrol station where you get £3 a day, 5 days a week.

Inland Revenue

PAYE

Reference: /

Coding claim

Please read these notes before you write anything:

Your employer has given you this form because you have not given him form P45. Without a P45 you may pay the wrong tax. If you can get a P45, you need not fill in this form. So
- if you left a job recently and have not since then claimed unemployment benefit, ask your old employer for a P45
- if you have been claiming unemployment benefit, sign off by returning card UB40. A P45 will then be sent to you.

You should however fill in this form
- if you cannot get a P45, or you have lost it or
- if this is your first paid job.

It will help you to get a correct PAYE code so that you pay the right tax. You may not have to fill in all of it. Please follow the instructions printed in blue and fill in those sections that apply to you, using CAPITAL letters.

A Everyone should fill in this section

Your surname .... Mr/Mrs/Miss/Ms.................

Your first names ....

Your new employer's name and address ....

The description or title of your new job ....

Your National Insurance number [ ][ ][ ][ ][ ]

Is this new job your **only** job? Please say YES or NO [ ]

If you have a second job, or do part-time or evening work, any payments you receive are part of your income. They are liable to tax in just the same way as the earnings from your regular job.

If your answer is 'YES', please turn to page 2. If your answer is 'NO', please fill in section B below.

B Please give details of any other work for which you get paid:

The description or title of the job ....
Your employer's name and address ....

If you work for yourself please write 'self-employed' ....

Your works/payroll number (if any) ....

Your tax reference (if known) ....

The branch or site where you work ....

Your total weekly earnings from the work before any stoppages £ ....

Which is your **main** job? Is it your new job, shown in section A? Or the job shown in section B?
Please write A or B [ ]

If your answer is 'A', please turn to page 2.
If your answer is 'B', please turn straight to page 4: there is no need to fill in pages 2 and 3.

SPECIMEN

P15   Page 1

Revision

1 Complete these sentences. Choose a word from the words in brackets.
a A person who employs you is an _____ (employer/employee)
b Punctual means _____. (prompt/prospects)
c A literate person is good at _____ (numbers/reading)
d Money taken away from gross pay is called _____ (an induction/a deduction)
e A contract is _____ (an agreement/a bonus)

2 What is the meaning of:
a PAYE _____?
b Clocking on _____?
c Piecework _____?
d Sickness benefit _____?
e Prospects _____?

3 Complete these words:
a class____ic__tions
b ab____it____s
c char____t____istics
d un____ploy____nt
e su____leme____ary
f ph__s____al
g occ____a____on
h app____ntice____ip
i in____ct____n
j li____r____e

4 Look at the list of learnt abilities on page 7. Which are needed by the following?
a Van driver _____
b Dressmaker _____
c Mechanic _____
d Photographer _____
e Poster designer _____

5 On page 5 we talked about good and bad points. What are the good and bad points of these jobs?

	Good	Bad
a Bricklayer		
b Clerk		
c Firefighter		
d Nurse		
e Factory worker		

6 You leave school at Easter. April 2nd is Easter Monday. Do you know when you should apply for benefit if you are unemployed? _____
If not, who would be able to tell you? _____

7 Name two jobs for each of these interest classifications:
a Artistic _____
b Computational _____
c Literary _____
d Practical _____
e Persuading/influencing _____

8 Name three indoors jobs that have good prospects and do not require uniform: _____

9 On page 7 we talked about characteristics. What personal characteristics have you got that an employer would like? Write them here:

_____
_____
_____

10 On page 7 we also talked about physical characteristics. Describe your physical characteristics here:

_____
_____

11 Write here three learnt abilities that you have:

_____
_____
_____

12 Now you are at the end of Unit 1. You should have thought about your interests, abilities and characteristics. You will have given some thought, too, to certain types of jobs.

　　Think of three jobs you would like and which would suit you. Write down the physical characteristics, learnt abilities and personal characteristics the jobs need.

_____
_____
_____

Explain why you think these jobs would suit you:

_____
_____
_____

Unit 2 Job hunting

Getting a job at all is difficult these days. There may be some jobs outside YTS. However, many school-leavers will start working life as trainees. They will be in Youth Training A or B Schemes rather than in a permanent job. Only after such a scheme will they really be on the job market.

To get a job or training scheme place, certain skills are useful. Whether an employee or trainee, you will probably need reading, writing and self-presentation skills. This unit will help you with these skills. It covers finding a job or training place that interests you. It helps prepare you for answering questions at interviews. It should help those who leave school without jobs or training places. It should also help those who leave YTS without a permanent job.

Help with job hunting (or with getting a YTS place) Who can help?	**16**
Applying for the Youth Training Scheme (YTS) A plan of action	**18**
Situations vacant ads Replying to ads	**20**
Answering ads Applying by letter and telephone	**22**
Making the first move Job enquiries	**25**
Application forms Filling in forms	**28**
The interview How to prepare	**30**
Leaving school and after Registering for a job	**32**
Revision	**34**

Help with job hunting (or with getting a YTS place)

Jobs these days are in short supply. Also, training scheme places that interest you may be limited in number. It is important, therefore, to make the most of the opportunities that you have. The exercises in this section provide help with job hunting or getting a YTS place.

*Read the **Words you need.** Think about the information presented. Then answer the questions.

Words you need

community   group of people or the public in general
correspondence course   lectures, notes and essays sent by post
options   choices

recruitment   obtaining new members
reference   a written statement about your work
voluntary   freely done; work without pay

SUE wants to go into hotel management or the Navy. She has a place at a sixth-form college for September which she would rather not take up, but she accepts that this is probably her best option. 'I've given up looking for a job,' she said. 'There are only YTS places. I wrote some letters asking for clerical work, but the Gas and Electricity Boards were the only ones that replied. They had no vacancies. Girls can't enter the Navy until they're $17\frac{1}{2}$. I just gave up. I said that's it – college.'

NICKY hoped to get into the RAF. He was disappointed when they told him that they were now not accepting people under 17 or 18. Nicky says: 'I felt desperate. I could see September coming, and me with no real job in my sights. My mum kept pushing me to go to the Careers Office. So I went about twice a week. I said I'd have a go at YTS for something to do. Then, one day I went to the Careers Office and there was one job. It was in engineering, making cutting tools. It's not a great job but I feel much better. I'm on the way up.'

MARITA wanted to work in a children's home rather than study child care at college. She found out they won't take on anyone under 18. 'I've got to go to college,' she said. 'Still, I'm getting used to the idea. Last week I went to the college – it was good. They're doing all the things I like. You get to work in different homes, so you can find out what you really want to do.'

ANDREW hoped for a craft apprenticeship. When he was interviewed by the Careers Officer he was interested to hear about YTS places in engineering works and at the local college. He starts with a firm in September. 'It seemed like second best at first,' said Andrew. 'Later, I learned more about it and I've changed my mind. There will be time for college study as well as experience in the factory. I might even get a certificate at the end of it. Of course, there's no guarantee of a job at the end. I believe that the firm hopes to take some trainees on. So I suppose it's up to me. Anyway, I've got something to do in September.'

? Questions

1 How did Sue try to get a job? _____

2 What seems to be Sue's best option? _____

3 Marita wants to work in a children's home. At what age will they take her? _____

4 According to Nicky, recruitment to the RAF starts at what age? _____

5 If often pays to keep on trying. How did Nicky keep on trying? _____

6 What did Andrew feel about YTS at first? _____

How does he feel now? _____

7 You overhear the following conversation:
   TOM: It's no good looking for a job. There aren't any. I'll pop in to the Careers Office every six months. I'm not taking anything without prospects.
   JOHN: I'm looking everywhere – in the papers, shop windows, Careers Office – and I'm asking friends and relations And if there's a YTS place that will give me the opportunity to follow the job I want, I'll take that.
   Who do you agree with? _____ Why? _____

8 An employer is interviewing Jane and Sally. Sally has just finished YTS. She has a nationally recognized certificate to show her progress and abilities as a worker. Jane has been unemployed since she left school twelve months ago (the same time as Sally).
   What might influence the employer to give the job to Sally?
   _____

Job hunting

9 Don't waste time if you haven't got a permanent job. You could gain good experience by following some of the options below. Fill in some of the things you could do.
   a Attending a full-time training course _____
   b Going to evening classes _____
   c Doing a correspondence course _____
   d Doing voluntary work at home _____
   e Doing voluntary work overseas _____
   f Learning skills from relatives or friends (e.g. decorating; driving a car) _____

10 What sort of job hunting help will I need?
   Help in deciding what jobs might interest me? Yes/No _____
   Help in getting information about different jobs? Yes/No _____
   Help in knowing what sorts of jobs are available? Yes/No _____
   Help in applying for the sort of job I want? Yes/No _____
   Any other sort of help? _____

11 Discuss with a friend: 'Who can help us find jobs?'

Applying for the Youth Training Scheme (YTS)

Many applications for places on YTS will be made through the Careers Service before you leave school. This may be the best time to apply as more places will probably be available. So how do you go about it? The exercises here will help you develop a 'plan of action'.

*Read the **Words you need**. Then study the 'plan of action' and answer the questions.

Words you need

Admissions Officer person who deals with applications for entry to college
application form the form you fill in to apply for a job or scheme
available to be had; within reach
Careers Service department set up to advise young people on careers
Personnel Officer person who interviews and hires staff
Project Leader person in charge of a project or scheme

Plan of action for YTS

1 Decide what sort of scheme might suit you. (What type of work? Based with a firm/a college/a community scheme?) Look back at Unit 1, pages 2, 4 and 5. If you can't decide, go on to number 2.
2 See your Careers Officer. (You should know the Careers Officer's name and address.) He/she can let you know about schemes and help you decide.
3 Use the other helpers that you have discussed (page 17, questions 10 and 11) to find out all you can about schemes.
4 Find out *who to apply to* **a** through the Careers Office;
 b directly to the firm, college or community project.
5 Find out *how* to apply **a** by letter (see page 22);
 b by application form (see page 28);
 c by interview (see page 30).
6 Make your application – and good luck!

Interviewing for a YTS place

Most applications for a YTS place will involve you in being interviewed. Here, much of what is covered on pages 30 and 31 will be important.

Look at these pages now. Then form some questions you would ask about YTS in an interview. Talk these over with a friend.

? Questions

1 Some questions you might ask about YTS are:
'What will I be doing?'
'What will I get at the end of two years?'
'Is there any chance of a permanent job at the end?'
Write three more questions you would like answers to below:

2 Who will be the best person to ask about YTS places?

3 When is the best time to apply for YTS?

4 How are YTS placements likely to be made?

5 In writing for a YTS place, is your writing important? Why?

6 If you phone for information on a Community Project who would you ask to speak to?

7 What is the form on which you apply for a job called?

8 What does it mean when you are told 'a place is not available'?

9 What is the title of the person who would interview you for a college course?

10 Who could interview you for a job in a factory?

11 Name three ways of applying for a YTS place:

12 You obtain a YTS place with a firm. Then you hear that the firm is closing down. What will you do?

Things to do

1 Interview some friends who are on YTS courses. Ask them how they applied for places. Ask them what they think is the best way to apply. Ask them what tips they can offer you.
2 Practise your skills at letter writing.
3 Practise interviewing and being interviewed with a friend.
4 Practise your telephone conversation with a Project Leader*.

Note: The rest of this Unit, while talking about jobs, helps with skills which are just as important when applying for YTS.

*Project Leaders could have a variety of names, e.g. Training Officer, Scheme Supervisor.

Situations vacant ads

The newspaper is one place to start job hunting. Get to know the *classified advertisements* section of your newspaper. Learn the skills involved in using newspaper ads. This section will help you.

*Read the **Words you need** carefully. Cover their meanings with your hand. Do you know them? Practise covering and uncovering them until you do. Then study the ads taken from newspapers. Answer the questions.

Words you need

applicant person who applies for a job
appointment arrangement to meet *or* a position in a firm
aptitude test test to see if you are suited to a job
canvasser person who goes around asking people's opinions
classified ads short advertisements arranged according to subject
commission percentage of sales
financial concerned with money
inexperienced lacking practice; not experienced
negotiable can be settled or changed
permanent long-term; lasting
phrase part of a sentence; a few words
salary wages, usually paid monthly
selection choice; picking out
temporary short-term

Look at these ads taken from a newspaper. Sometimes they are grouped under 'Situations Vacant'. Some newspapers group them under 'General Vacancies' or just 'Jobs'. These are permanent jobs. There may also be 'Temporary' or 'Part-time Vacancies' sections. Sometimes temporary or part-time jobs can lead to permanent ones. The ads here are a mixture of 'General' and 'Part-time' Vacancies.

1

TELEPHONE SALES STAFF

are required by the Liverpool Mail to work in our New Street offices.
It is unlikely that anyone under the age of 18 would be considered capable of fulfilling this demanding role.
Applicants should be educated to G.C.E. 'O' level standard, but most of all should be bright and alert with persuasive personality.
Previous sales experience will be an advantage but sales training will be given.
It will be necessary for applicants to undertake aptitude tests prior to final selection.
We offer a basic salary of £4,435 p.a. plus bonus, good working conditions and the opportunity for career development.
Apply in the first instance by writing to
SUSANNAH BROWNLOW
PERSONNEL OFFICER,

LIVERPOOL MAIL LIMITED,
P.O. Box 4,
New Street,
Liverpool.

2

YOUR CAREER

IF YOU ARE LOOKING FOR A

GOOD WAGE

IF YOU ARE INEXPERIENCED OR

Looking for something new

IF YOU ARE

18 - 25

AND EAGER TO WORK AND
LOOKING FOR A JOB TELEPHONE STRAIGHT AWAY

051-970 6311

(up to 6 p.m.)

3 **HAIRDRESSER** required, full or part-time. Phone 051-228 4472 (day), or 051-751 5848 (evenings).

4 **FINANCIAL** Assistant required for part-time job involving book-keeping, preparation of accounts, and pay roll management, for small company near central Liverpool; short term appointment only but must be able to start immediately. Call 051-096 8236.

5 **EXPERIENCED** Part-time Office Help required for small company in the Woolton area, must be able to handle straight-forward bookkeeping, wages and typing, hours to suit. If interested, please phone 02775 2811.

6 **JOINERS** required for varied and interesting work, Merseyside area, good rates of pay and bonus scheme in operation. Box PBG 47 Mail.

7 **NON-EXPERIENCED** Canvassers wanted, top rates. 051-271 8362.

20

? Questions

1. Write down the numbers of the ads which mention part-time work.

2. If you want to apply for the job of hairdresser, you phone

   _____ (day)
   _____ (evening)

3. Look at number 1. The salary for this job per week is roughly
   a £65; **b** £70; **c** £75; **d** £85

4. In number 1, what is thought to be more important than 'O' levels?

5. One phrase in 1 indicates good career prospects. Write it down here.

6. Number 1 offers more than a basic salary. What words suggest this?

7. How will applicants for 1 be finally selected?

8. Write down the address you need to apply for the joiner's job.

9. In which of the ads is experience not necessary?

10. Write down the first three words of the ad concerning bookkeeping.

11. Which job is advertising a temporary appointment?

12. In how many of the ads should you reply by telephone?

13. A personnel officer may be the person you reply to. What is the name of the personnel officer in number 1?

14. Sometimes employers do not ask you to write to their address. They ask you to write to a Box Number. The newspaper keeps a numbered box in their office for such mail. Why do you think employers would want to use box numbers?

15. Which ads leave you wanting to know more?

16. If a canvasser is paid by commission, would he push sales? Why?

17. Number 4 says 'hours to suit'. What does this mean?

18. Number 4 is looking for a clerk with experience. A girl has been helping out in the school office. She has done a clerical course at school. Should she apply for this job? Why?

An ad to suit me

19. Think of a job you would like. Think of the abilities and characteristics you have. Add any other good points an employer might like. Now write out an ad to suit yourself. Put down the salary and as much information as you think necessary. Don't forget to put the address or phone number of the employer.

Answering ads

Writing a letter of application

Ads often ask you to write to a person or a company. From the letters received the employer decides who should be interviewed. Those selected for an *interview* are on the employer's 'short list'. Can you see how important your letter is? It could get you included on the short list. Will the employer want to interview you? A lot depends on your letter.

The exercises here will help you write a letter of application. Learn how to do this. You may have many such letters to write in the future.

*Read the **Words you need** carefully. Study the letter of application and the tips for writing it. Then answer the questions.

Words you need

closing ending of a letter, e.g. Yours sincerely/Yours faithfully
convenience suitable time
interview formal meeting with a person asking questions
letter of application letter applying for a job
signature the way you sign your name

Tips

Include all parts A–G shown in Jean's letter. Remember your letter is a chance to get an interview.

> (A) 25 Palace Road,
> Seaforth,
> Lancs. L30 3SU
> (B) 20 July 1983
>
> (C) Manager,
> Seaforth Toys,
> Seaforth,
> Lancs.
>
> (D) Dear Sir/Madam,
> (E) I would like to apply for the post of Clerical Assistant, advertised in 'The Echo' on 18 July.
> I am sixteen years old and left Seaforth High School this summer. I am awaiting my GCE/CSE examination results.
> One of my options at school was Typing and Secretarial Work. Last term I worked one day a week in the school office. I also did office work at weekends in a children's home.
> The Principal of the home has kindly agreed to give a reference if required. His address is: Crosby Home, Seaforth Road, Crosby.
> I would be pleased to attend an interview at your convenience.
> (F) Yours faithfully,
> (G) Jean Roberts

A Your address in full
B Date
C Name and address of the person/company you are writing to
D Greeting (if you don't know the person's name, use *Dear Sir/Madam*)
E Content of the letter:
  1 job applied for
  2 schools attended
  3 results of any exams
  4 experience/interests
  5 why you should be considered
F A formal closing
G Your signature

+ Your letter should be polite, clear and to the point.
+ Use good quality paper and write in ink or type it.
+ Your letter should be clean and neat. All words should be spelt correctly.
+ If in doubt, use a dictionary. Or ask someone who is a good speller to check your letter.
+ Write out your letter in rough first. Keep the rough copy to remind you what you wrote.

? Questions

1 Look at advert 1 on page 20. What greeting would you use in your reply?
   Dear ....

2 Why should you write out a letter in rough first?
   _____
   _____

3 The tips on page 22 tell us to use good writing paper. Some people use paper out of old exercise books to write letters of application. What do you think of their chances of an interview?
   _____
   _____

4 Jean Roberts's letter is in answer to an advertisement. Imagine that you want to apply for this job. Answer these questions:

   a What is your complete address?
   _____ (Tip A)
   _____
   _____
   _____

   b When are you writing this letter?
   _____ (Tip B)

   c To whom should you address the letter? (Their name and address)
   _____ (Tip C)
   _____
   _____

   d How should you write the greeting?
   _____ (Tip D)

   e Why are you writing? Write the first sentence of your letter.
   _____ (Tip E)
   _____
   _____

   f What closing will you use?
   _____ (Tip F)

5 Write your signature here:
   _____

6 Write down the five things we have said should be in the 'Content' of the letter.
   _____
   _____
   _____
   _____
   _____

7 Look at advert 5 on page 20. How would you write the greeting?
   _____

8 Write out a letter of application for the job you described on page 21. Write it on a separate piece of paper. Remember to use the tips from page 22.

9 On the envelope below, write the address for mailing your letter.

Answering ads by telephone

Sometimes you may have to telephone for an application form. Many ads tell you to phone in reply. Usually the name of the person to contact is given. But not always! In any case, be prepared to speak clearly, *relevantly* and politely. The company you phone may have a *telephone answering machine*. The machine records what you say but cannot hold a conversation. So, you should have your information written down in front of you.

The exercises in this unit and this checklist will help you. You should not be stuck for words when you telephone.

*Read the **Words you need**. Study the advert and the checklist. Then answer the questions.

Words you need

cert. certificate
mature grown up
personnel the staff of a firm
relevantly to the point

surgery a room where advice or treatment, usually medical, is given
telephone answering machine machine that tape-records incoming calls

Here is an advert from the 'Mail' of August 10th.

> **PERSONNEL** Clerk to be trained for work in office and surgery of small firm. First aid cert. helpful. Phone 312 5652.

Below is a **Getting prepared checklist**. Write down the answers you would make if applying for this job.

Getting prepared checklist

1 What do you need *before* ringing up?
- the phone number
- enough change if using a call box _____ (What coins?)
- pen and paper for interview details if offered (e.g. time and place)

2 What do you need to say?
- title of the job
- who to ask for (person or firm)
- where you saw the job advertised
- details about yourself that the employer will want to know (name/age/school/exams)
- other things about yourself that will help your application (experience, interests, etc.)

3 Make sure you ask about:
- training you might get
- prospects (what you can expect)
- people you would be working with
- how much you will earn
- what hours you will work

4 Say when you are available for interview (or work).

5 Ask if there is anything else about the job you should know:
- transport, special clothes, etc.

Making the first move

These days many jobs never get advertised. Why? Because so many people, especially school-leavers, are chasing so few jobs. People who approach the firms themselves may get some jobs. What does it mean if jobs are not looking for you? It means you must go to look for the jobs!
   The following exercises will help you in making job *enquiries*.

*Read the **Words you need**. Study the information on enquiring. Look at the section from Yellow Pages. Then answer the questions.

Words you need

contractors   firm that provides building supplies
domestic   for the home
enquiring   making enquiries; asking questions; investigating
industrial   relating to manufacture or trade
installations   equipment in buildings for lighting, etc.
positive pestering   constantly and politely asking until you get what you want
Yellow Pages   phone book of local businesses under headings

Enquiring – where to start

You probably know some types of employer in your town or neighbourhood already. You probably know the big shops and businesses, for example. But there may be others you are interested in. How do you find out about these?
   You could find out – through the Careers Office
                     – through friends and relatives
                     – through Yellow Pages.
Remember. Many industrial employers will also have office and warehouse staff.
   Here is an extract from Yellow Pages. It is part of one of many pages concerning electrical contractors.

Chesworth A, 8 Jeffereys Dv, Huyton 051-521 4891
Christian F, 41 Walton La 4 .... 051-525 9505
Clark & Bligh (Electrical) Ltd—
   Colonsay Ho, Crosby Rd Sth 22 .... 051-263 6491

CLARK & BLIGH Ltd.
SPECIALISTS IN INDUSTRIAL
ELECTRICAL INSTALLATIONS
Commercial & Private
2 Balliol Road, Huyton
Liverpool L20 7EH   051-678 6788

CLARKE WM (ELECTRICAL CONTRS) Ltd.
621 Westminster Rd 051-339 3211

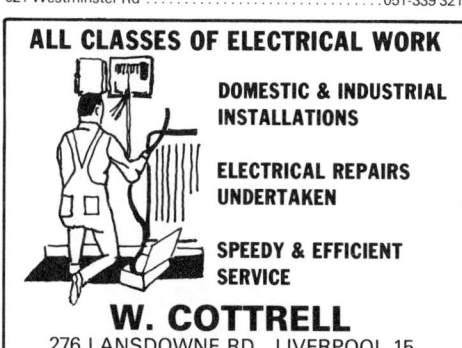

ALL CLASSES OF ELECTRICAL WORK
DOMESTIC & INDUSTRIAL INSTALLATIONS
ELECTRICAL REPAIRS UNDERTAKEN
SPEEDY & EFFICIENT SERVICE
W. COTTRELL
276 LANSDOWNE RD., LIVERPOOL 15
051-486 4881

With this information you can
– telephone (you have the phone number)
– write (you have the address)
– call in (you have the address)

? Questions

1 Clark & Bligh can be contacted at two phone numbers. What are they?

2 What does W. Cottrell do besides installations?

3 Wm. Clarke has a shortened version of 'contractors' after his name. Write it here:

4 In alphabetical order, who would be the first contractor you see?

A telephone enquiry

Remember the **Getting prepared checklist** on page 24? Let's use this to telephone W. Cottrell (page 25). Write your answers on the lines:

1 What do I need *before* ringing up?   (phone number) _____

_____

_____

2 What do I need to know?
 – (job title);
 – (whom I want to speak to – if it's a big firm, the Personnel Officer).

_____

_____

_____

3 What I need to ask: full details about any jobs that may be on offer; how I can apply for any jobs that are going.

_____

_____

_____

*Remember: be polite, interested and relevant.

A letter of enquiry

Remember the letter of application on page 22? Letters of enquiry require a similar approach. But there are some important differences:

- You have to decide to *whom* to address the letter.
- You have to identify the *type* of work you are interested in (remember no job has been advertised).
- You have to decide what are the *most relevant things* to say about yourself. In the space below, write a letter of enquiry to Wm. Clarke for a job. The letter of application on page 22 may help with this.

Personal enquiry

This means going to the employer and asking about a job. Will employers like this? Some may not, particularly if they are busy. But others may feel it shows enthusiasm – a good point. There is no way of learning how to handle personal enquiry except through practice. When you do this, bear in mind three things:
- whom to ask for;
- what to ask about;
- how to ask.

? Questions

1 I enquire at the office of a big firm. For whom should I ask?

2 I should have the _____ of the job in mind when I enquire.

3 Name two things you could ask about.

4 What should you take with you?

Following up enquiries

Some firms may say that a job may be coming up. They are not too sure. Ask them when they will know. Ask if you can contact them again at that time. Keeping in touch like this is important – we call it 'positive pestering'! Again, there is no substitute for practice at this. For example, imagine you have received this letter:

Dear _____,

Thank you for your enquiry. Although we have no vacancies at present, we may have one in the summer. If you are interested in this, please contact us then.

Yours faithfully,

T. Smith (Miss)
Personnel Officer

? Questions

5 You could respond to this at once in three ways:

6 If you reply by letter, write this out below:
Dear _____,

Yours

7 When would you contact the firm again?
- beginning of summer
- middle of summer
- end of summer?

8 How would it be best to make this contact?

9 Write out the first thing you would say if phoning:

Application forms

The way you fill in application forms says a lot about you. A complete, neatly written job application form may impress the employer. It could show that your work is always neat and complete. Words crossed or rubbed out may suggest the opposite. Perhaps your work is careless, or you change you mind a lot. Follow the tips below. Make your filled-in form work for you, instead of against you.

*Read the **Words you need** carefully. Study the tips for filling in forms. Then answer the questions.

Words you need

application written request for a job
legibly clearly; able to be read
maiden name woman's name before marriage
occupation job; employment
particulars details
previous before; earlier
reference a statement about you by a person who knows you

Tips

- First read through the form carefully before starting to write.
- Always print or type.
- Answer all questions and fill in all blanks. Some questions may not apply to you. If so, write N/A in the blank (N/A means 'not applicable', 'does not apply').
- Some forms have boxes for your answers. You have to put a tick in the boxes.
- Spell all words correctly.
- Are there some words you don't understand? Check them in a dictionary or ask someone for help.
- Your signature is the way you *sign* your name. Do not print your signature.

  A B C D E F G H I J K L M N O P Q R S T U V W X Y Z — Capitals

  a b c d e f g h i j k l m n o p q r s t u v w x y z — Small letters

? Questions

1 Print the alphabet in block (capital) letters below at A.
   Print the alphabet in small letters at a.
   Compare with the samples given above.

   A _____

   a _____

2 Your date of birth is 14th December 1968. You write this on the form as 14/12/68.
   How would you write 3rd January 1969?

3 An employer does not want references to be from your friends and relatives. Why not?

4 Fill in the form opposite. You are applying for the position of salesperson. Your previous employment was as a part-time salesperson. Make up a name and address for this employer. Make all personal details on the form refer to yourself. Use N/A if necessary.

Application for Employment Private and confidential

PERSONAL DETAILS (Please use block letters)

Surname	First names	Maiden name (if applicable)

Present address	Telephone No.	Nat. Ins. No.

Date of birth	Place of birth	Nationality	Married, single, divorced or widowed	Number and ages of children

POSITION APPLIED FOR ....

EDUCATION AND TRAINING

	Name	Dates attended		Examinations passed
		From	To	
School				

PARTICULARS OF PREVIOUS EMPLOYMENT

Name and address of employer ....
....
Date started........................... Date left........................... Weekly wages...........................
Nature of work ....
Reason for leaving ....

PERSONAL REFERENCES

Name	Address	Occupation	Known how long

Date .... Signature...

The interview

Your telephone call, letter or personal enquiry has been made. Your application has won you an interview. This is your chance to make an *impression*. You could persuade the employer that you are suitable. So prepare to show yourself off in the best possible light. During the interview you will be asked many questions. Your ability to give *relevant* answers can help you to be successful. Prepare well for the interview – getting the job depends on it.

Work in this section will help you to get ready for interviews.

*Read the **Words you need** carefully. Study the tips. Then answer the questions.

Words you need

impression what you seem to be like to someone who meets you
prospects chances of getting on
receptionist office person who deals with enquiries/visitors
relevant to the point; directly related to the subject
techniques skilled ways of doing things
vet (veterinary) to do with the medical treatment of animals

Tips

- *Be suitably dressed.* You would not wear a suit for the job of labourer. Would you wear old jeans for a job in an office? Generally, aim to be clean, neat and well groomed.
- *Be prepared.* Before interview, remind yourself what you said when you applied. Look again at your letter of application. Take school certificates or reports that may interest the employer.
- *Be on time.* Find out where the employer is. Plan the route and give yourself plenty of time to get there.
- *Make sure* you take the name of the person to ask for. Note the telephone number so that you can phone if you are delayed.
- *Be relaxed.* This is easier said than done. It pays to get as much interviewing practice as you can. Practise both at school and outside.
- *Be interested.* This is the only chance you have. Ask questions that show your interest. Look back to Unit 1, pages 4–5. This will remind you of some important factors in considering jobs.
- *Be polite* and speak clearly.
- *Be relevant* and enthusiastic.

? Questions

> **Positions Vacant**
> **SALES ASSISTANT**
>
> Record shop in Vale Centre. Some sales experience preferred, but not essential. For interview phone Mr Block: 567 6624

1 Suppose you are being interviewed for this job as a sales assistant. Imagine all the answers under each question are true for you. Tick the most *relevant* answers to the questions.

a What kind of work have you done?
- ☐ I have worked as a part-time salesperson at Adams'.
- ☐ I have been a baby sitter and competition swimmer.
- ☐ I have collected records for years.

b Why are you interested in working in this shop?
- ☐ All my friends come in here, and I'd enjoy seeing them often.
- ☐ I need a job, and you have a vacancy.
- ☐ I like records and know that I would enjoy selling them.

> **CASHIER**
>
> Trainee cashier needed at Drew's Discount Store. Junior. Reliable. Good at figures. Opportunities for advancement. For appointment phone: 397 4210

2 Suppose that you are being interviewed for this job as a cashier. All the answers listed under each question are true for you. Choose the most relevant answer for each question.

a What makes you think you could do a good job?
- ☐ I learn fast, and I'm good at maths.
- ☐ I like handling money.
- ☐ I type accurately.

b How did you do at school?
- ☐ Very well. Would you like to see my last report?
- ☐ Art was my best subject.
- ☐ Better than average. I wasn't a genius, but I did my best.

c What do you hope to be eventually?
- ☐ I hope to be a very rich person.
- ☐ I've always wanted to be a champion tennis player.
- ☐ I want to be someone with a good job in sales.

> **PART-TIME** kennel help. Also evening and weekend receptionist. For vet. Clinic. Phone 368 2812.

3 Think of three questions that you would like to ask about the job described in this advert. Write them on the lines below.

a _____
_____

b _____
_____

c _____
_____

Leaving school and after

There are many people who try to find work for school-leavers. Despite their efforts, some will be without a job or YTS place to go to. So, what steps do you take if you have no job or training scheme place? Most school-leavers want to register for a job or place on a scheme. They can also register for any benefits they are entitled to. (What are benefits? See Unit 1 page 10.)

The exercises here will help you in registering. They will help you to know those benefits you are entitled to.

*Read the **Words you need** carefully. Follow the chart below and complete it. Then answer the questions.

Words you need

DHSS Department of Health and Social Security
registering signing on
UBO Unemployment Benefit Office
YTS Youth Training Scheme

Registering for work and benefits chart

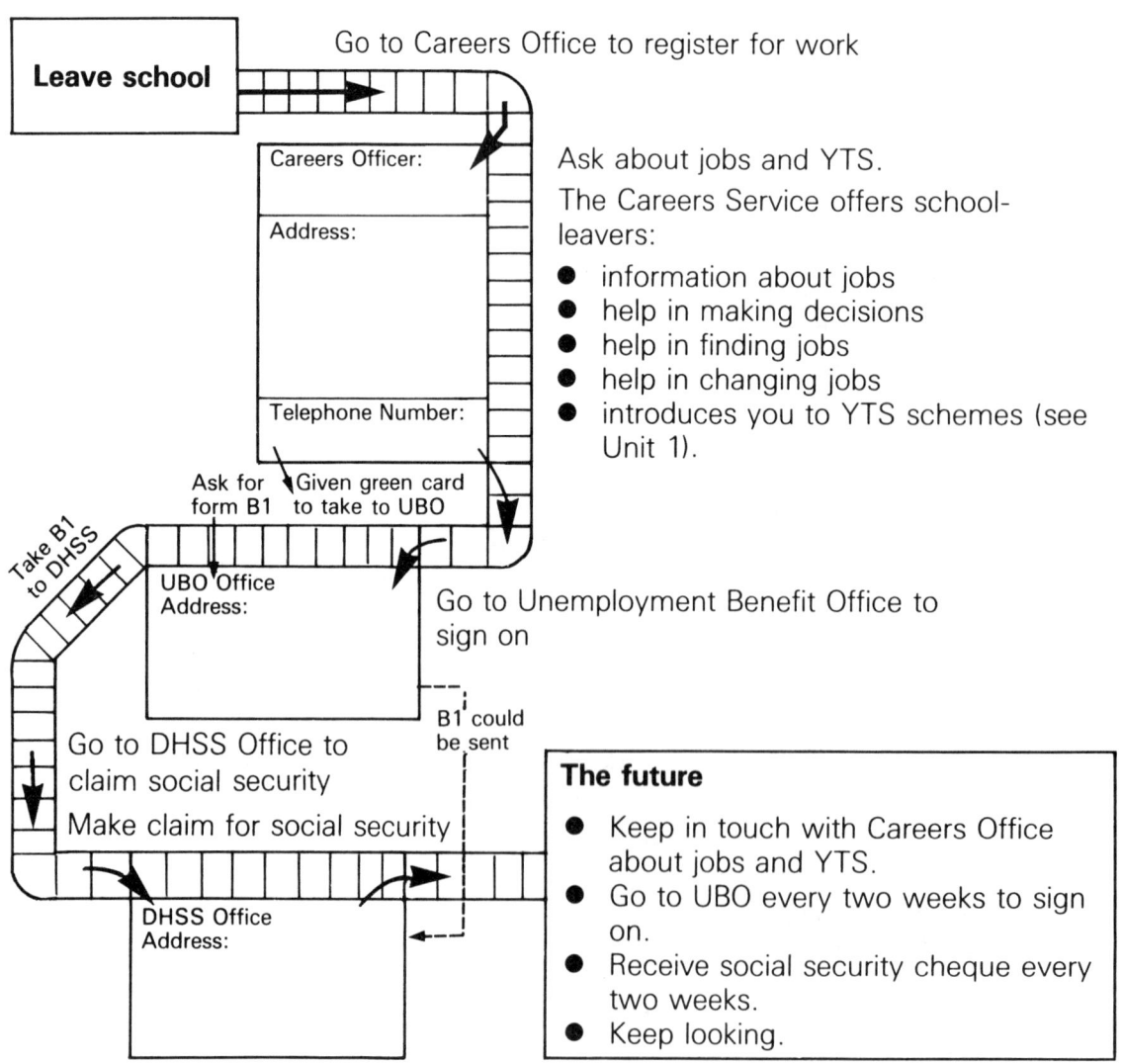

? Questions

1. Suppose you were out of work. Where would you claim social security?
   _____

2. Write down here three things the Careers Officer can help you do:
   _____
   _____
   _____

3. Where do you sign on?
   _____

4. What do you take from the Careers Office to the UBO?
   _____

5. What is the name of the form that you take to the DHSS for social security?
   _____

6. How often should an unemployed person sign on at the UBO?
   _____

7. How much is the social security benefit? **a** at 16? **b** at 18?
   a _____ **b** _____

8. You want special help with an interview, or information on a job. Should you go to the UBO, YTS, Careers Office or DHSS?
   _____

9. Where would you cash a cheque for social security?
   _____

10. If you are out of work, why keep in touch with the Careers Office?
    _____
    _____

11. You are ill. You cannot get to the UBO. What should you do?
    _____
    _____

12. If you find work, should you inform anybody? Who?
    _____

13. The following information is about registering for work and benefits. But it is all jumbled up. Sort out the order in which these happen. Put them in order in the right-hand column:
    - go to the UBO to sign on
    - leave school
    - keep in touch with Careers Office
    - go to the DHSS with form B1
    - take green card to the UBO
    - go to the Careers Office to register

    1. _____
    2. _____
    3. _____
    4. _____
    5. _____
    6. _____

Revision

1 Write out the meanings for the following words:
   a option _____
   b voluntary _____
   c commission _____
   d temporary _____
   e guarantee _____
   f permanent _____
   g negotiable _____

2 When job hunting, we suggested that you keep asking politely. What name did we give this?
   P_____ p_____

3 Write out the following abbreviations in full:
   a cert. _____
   b MSC _____
   c ads/adverts _____
   d vet _____
   e YTS _____
   f N/A _____

4 When we gave tips for interview techniques, we suggested eight things. Name four of them:
   _____ _____
   _____ _____

Look at these ads and answer questions 5–15.

A
CLERK
Reliable. Some experience of general office duties. Good prospects; excellent facilities.
Phone: Personnel Officer, Betty Stevens, for interview 9 a.m.–6 p.m. – 289 1689

B
CLERK
General Duties
One year's experience at least. Starting salary £2750. Good phone manner. Able to deal with important clients. Apply in writing to:
Mr S. Donovan, Personnel, Legal Trust Ltd, 2 Penn Rd, Nottingham.

5 Which ad (A or B) gives details of salary?

6 You are interested in job A. Between what times should you phone?

7 How much per week (roughly) is ad B offering?

8 Name two advantages of ad A which are not mentioned in ad B.

9 To whom will you address the letter of application for ad B?

10 What is the name of the personnel officer in ad A?

11 After you have asked for this person, what else will you say? Write down the next thing you will say:

12 We talked about answering ads by phone on pages 23–4. Think back. What questions would you want to ask the personnel officer (ad A)?

13 You wish to apply for the job with Legal Trust Ltd. Write the greeting and first sentence of your letter below:

14 Which of the jobs (ad A or B) would be more difficult to get?

Why? _____

15 Write down here three pieces of information you would ask Mr Donovan (ad B):

16 What does 'maiden name' on a form mean?

17 In helping with job hunting we talked about sources of help. Name four places to look for jobs:

18 How much money do you get paid as a trainee in YTS?

19 If you are travelling a long way to work on YTS, are you entitled to more money? What is the rule about this?

20 You will need plenty of practice in completing all sorts of forms. The form below is part of an application form for a bank clerk's job. Complete the form, including any information you need to make up. Do not leave any blanks.

Surname (in block letters)	Christian or Forenames	Mr Mrs Miss/Ms
Present address	Date of Birth	
Telephone Number	Place of Birth	
Maiden Name (if applicable)	Nationality	
Marital Status Single/Engaged/Married	Date of Marriage	Ages of children
Have you made any previous applications to join this Bank? Yes/No If yes, give details	What other occupations are you considering?	

Names of Schools or Colleges attended since the age of 11	Addresses	From Year	To Year

35

21 Write a brief letter to the manager of your local supermarket. Ask about part-time work as an assistant. Include all of the parts needed in a business letter.

22 Why do you think you should fill in application forms in capital letters? _____

23 After doing a YTS course, why should you register at the UBO again? _____

24 YTS includes *off the job* training, often at a local college. If this gives you the chance to study for a qualification, would you want to try for this?

Say why: _____

Unit 3 Office jobs

General office work can be a starting point for many interesting jobs. Other office jobs require special training. Whatever office jobs you do, you will need reading and writing skills. Many of these skills are important in other jobs too. Filing, taking messages, phoning, following directions, proofreading and letter writing are always useful. This unit is concerned with these skills.

Clerk 38
Filing skills

Receptionist/telephonist 40
Dealing with callers

Office machine operator 42
Using a copy machine

Typist 44
Proofreading; using hyphens

Secretary 46
Fact finding; Writing letters

Revision 48

Clerk

Clerks have to learn many skills. They may have to write, type and use machines. One skill they will have to learn is filing. Business papers need to be found quickly and easily. They are usually kept in files in *alphabetical* order. This makes them easy to find. Clerks may have to arrange and keep files in order. To begin with, you need to understand alphabetical order.

As a company grows, its filing system becomes more complex. Letters and other documents need to be filed under categories. As a clerk you may have to decide on the categories. Your skill in filing will help others to find information quickly. The exercises here will help you.

*Read the **Words you need** carefully. Study the information given. Then answer the questions.

Words you need

alphabetical in order from A to Z
article in grammar, the words *a, an* and *the*
chronologically in the order that things happen

correspondence letters
file folder for storing papers
memo memorandum (*plural*: memoranda), notes sent within a firm

Tips for filing

Look at the cards A, B and C.
  A Put names in alphabetical order by surname.
  B Surnames the same? Put in order by the first name.
  C Surnames begin with the same letter? Order by the second letter. First two letters the same? Go to the third letter.

Filing by category

- Get to know the categories in the cabinet.
- What kind of item are you filing? Is it a letter, report, account or a memo?
- Is there a key word in the heading?
- Sometimes you may need to skim through the item. Then you can decide which category it fits into.
- Generally there is a labelled folder for each category (put in alphabetical order).
- Dated material is filed chronologically with the most recent date first.

Filing by company name

- When the articles *a, an* or *the* are part of a company name – use the next word as the one to place in alphabetical order.

- When letters are part of the company name – place in alphabetical order according to the first letter.

- When numbers are part of the company name – place the name in alphabetical order as if the number was spelt.

The (H)eath Group
A (N)ew Image Ltd
(A)V Daydream Tours
(P) & S Home Constructions
Four (4) – Corners Company
(100) Hits Records Ltd — One hundred

? Questions

1 You work for a sales company. You have to sort the following files into alphabetical order. Write out the order here:

Price Lists   _____
Reports, Sales   _____
Memos, Sales   _____
Mailing Lists   _____
Price Increases   _____
Reports, Expense _____
Reports, Budget   _____
Memos, New Product _____
Clients, Overseas _____
Contracts, Clients' _____

2 You work for a firm of solicitors. You must put the files for these clients in order. Number them alphabetically.

Albert Gibbs   _____
The Maxwell Company   _____
Arthur Mason   _____
Louise Baker-Smith   _____
Dennis McMannis   _____
Jean Massey   _____
Geoffrey Massoni   _____
Gibson Homewares Ltd   _____
1-2-3-Floorcoverings   _____
A.J. Mason   _____

3 Letters with the following dates are filed in chronological order. Number them to show their order:
__ 12 Dec. 1980   __ 15/11/79
__ Feb. 6 1982   __ 8/9/80
__ 7 May 1981   __ 3 Sept. '82

4 Look at the file folders on page 38. Choose where you would file each of the following papers. Write the category on the line provided.

a Memo to all sales staff

b Pay rates for senior typists

c Order from Apex Ltd, France

d Sales report from London Office for 19/8/82–26/8/82

e A letter about the amount sold in 1981

5 You are helping out in a school office. You have been asked to find the items listed below. A list of the categories is given. Write the category under which each would be found.
Categories: MEDICAL; STUDENT RECORDS; RULES and PROCEDURES; APPLICATIONS.

a Health report forms

b Information sheet covering school field-trips

c Report card for Mary Brown, a student

d Mrs Turin's job application form

e Rules covering operation of the school canteen

Receptionist/telephonist

Taking telephone messages

Receptionists handle many telephone calls every day. They give information to callers and must know how to record information. They have to be good listeners. Receptionists have to ask the right questions. They must get all the important details and write them down accurately. We all need to take messages sometimes, at work or at home. It is important that we know how to do this properly.

The following exercises give practice in receiving and writing down messages.

*Read the **Words you need.** Study the information on taking messages. Then answer the questions.

Words you need

ext. extension
re about; concerning

urgent needing immediate attention
verify go over; check by repeating

Tips

- Have paper and pencil ready.
- Ask for the caller's name. Note the name of the person being called.
- Write down the caller's company, address, telephone number and dialling code.
- Ask the caller to spell all names you are unsure of.
- If you don't understand something, say so politely.
- Write down the important details of the message.
- Verify all information before the caller hangs up.

WHILE YOU WERE OUT

Recording the Details

- Who is the message for? — To: *Mark Stanford*
- When did the person call? — Date: *25/6* Time: *10.15* a.m.
- Who called? — M*rs* *Eileen Harrow*
  of *Tru - Art Studio*
- Where can the caller be reached? (Don't forget the dialling code.) — Phone: *051 213 356* Ext.: *—*

This is the most basic information.
- ☑ telephoned
- ☐ wanted to see you
- ☐ called to see you
- ☑ please call *(after 3)*
- ☐ will call again
- ☐ urgent

Keep the message brief and include only the important details.
- Message: *re Pete the Possum – children's book. Needs to know final page size*

- Who took the message? — Operator: *Sue Simon*

Speech bubbles:
- IS THERE SOMEONE ELSE WHO CAN HELP YOU?
- IS THAT ONE R OR TWO?
- COULD YOU SPELL THE COMPANY NAME PLEASE?
- WHEN CAN YOU BE REACHED AT THAT NUMBER?
- CAN I TAKE A MESSAGE PLEASE?

? Questions

1 Look at the message pad on the previous page.
  a Who is the message for? _____
  b Who is the message from? _____
  c What is the operator's name? _____
  d When should the call be returned? _____

2 As the receptionist, you take a call for Mr Herley. You inform the caller that Mr Herley is not in at the moment. The caller says, 'Oh well, thanks anyway.' What questions should you ask before the caller hangs up?

_____
_____
_____

3a You take a call for Mrs Stetson. The caller tells you his name and company. He wants his call returned as soon as possible. What is the first question you should ask?

_____

 b What is the second question you should ask?

_____

4 At 9.15 on 5 November, Rex took a message for Mr Greenway. It is shown on the right. This message may cause problems for him when he returns. List below all the reasons why the message may cause problems.

_____
_____
_____
_____
_____
_____
_____
_____

WHILE YOU WERE OUT

To _Brian Greenway_
Date _____ Time _____ a.m. / p.m.
M _Diane B._
of _____
Phone _351 9700_ Ext. _____

- ☑ telephoned
- ☐ wanted to see you
- ☐ called to see you
- ☑ please call
- ☐ will call again
- ☑ urgent

Message _Problem with new product you sent her. New client_
Operator _Rex_

5 Someone calls at the office to see Mr Herley. He won't be back in the office for an hour. You take the caller's name, address and telephone number. You ask what the caller wishes to see Mr Herley about. Are there any other things you can do for the caller? Are there any other questions you think should be asked?

_____
_____

Office machine operator

Most offices these days use all sorts of machines. There are accounting machines, visual display units, computers and copying machines. These need an operator. Sometimes a person will operate more than one kind of machine. Often, training for a machine can be done in two weeks. The more complicated machines, e.g. computers, take longer. Some employers seek operators with CSEs, but they're not always essential. Most operators are trained on the job.

The exercises in this section are about one type of machine used to duplicate papers. Copying machines are easy to operate. Just follow the instructions and read the diagrams carefully.

*Read the **Words you need**. Read the information given. Study the diagrams and answer the questions.

Words you need

accounting machines machines that work out costs and prices
duplicate make an exact copy
instructions directions for operating a machine
multiple many; more than one
original the item from which you make a copy
quantity the number
visual display unit (VDU) machine that displays information on a screen

? Questions

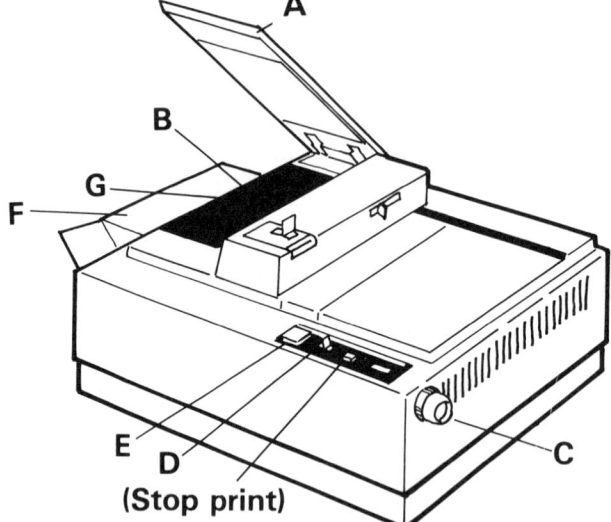
(Stop print)

1 Write the letter of the correct answer.
a How can you make the copies lighter or darker? _____
b Which step tells you how to place the original on the machine? _____
c Which button starts the machine copying? _____
d To make more than one copy, which step should you follow? _____
e Which part of the diagram is not mentioned in the instructions? _____

Copying Instructions
A Lift cover.
B Place original face down and close cover.
C Dial number of copies.
D Set light/dark lever.
E Press PRINT.
F Look for copies in tray.
G Lift cover and remove original.

2 Although copying machines may each be a little different, some operating steps are common to all. This diagram of another type of copying machine comes with an incomplete set of instructions. Complete each step.

a Press switch marked POWER ON.
b Lift _____
c Place original _____
d Close _____
e Set the _____ lever to the desired darkness.
f To make more than one copy, _____
g Press _____ button.
h Get copy or copies from _____
i Lift cover and _____
j Press switch marked _____

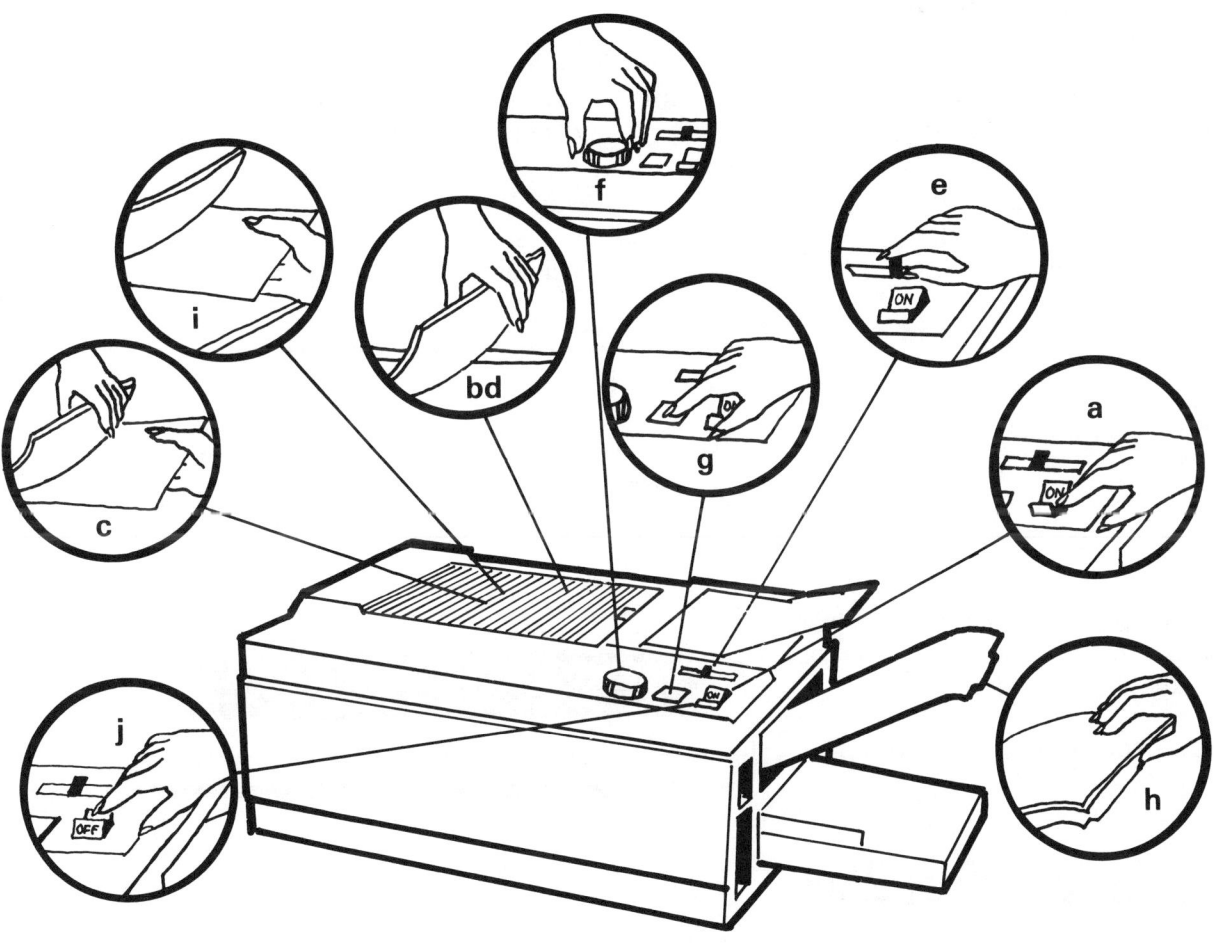

3 There is a lot of routine in machine operating. Some people may not like this. Can you think of some advantages of being a machine operator? Write them here:
_____
_____

4 It might help your prospects to learn how to operate several machines. Say why this might be so:
_____
_____

43

Typist

Typists need to learn many skills. Some of their skills are useful to all of us. *Proofreading* is one. They have to spot mistakes. They have to be able to pick up spelling and punctuation errors. Another skill is breaking words at the end of a line. This is done to get neat *margins*. For this it is necessary to *hyphenate* words. Knowing basic rules for this can be helpful to everyone.

The exercises in this section give help in learning these skills.

*Read the **Words you need**. Look at the information on proofreading and breaking words. Then answer the questions.

Words you need

hyphenate split up a word with a dash (-) called a 'hyphen'

margin space at the edge of a typed or written page

prefix word or syllable added in front of a word. This adds to or changes its meaning (e.g. 'un')

proofreading checking copy for errors

suffix word or syllable added at the end of a word. This makes another word, e.g. 'ness' added to 'sad' makes 'sadness'

syllables small units of sound into which words can be split

When you proofread, you look back and forth from the original to the typed copy to make sure they are both the same.

Can you spot the three mistakes?

Tips for proofreading
- Read slowly and carefully, checking each word.
- Proofread with your paper still in the typewriter. Roll back to the beginning of the sheet and compare the original with your copy, line by line.
- Use a dictionary if you need to check any spellings.

What to look for
- something omitted such as a punctuation mark, a word or even an entire sentence.
- misspelt words.
- incorrect punctuation, such as a comma instead of a full stop.
- correct form: Is the spacing similar? Are the paragraphs the same in both the original and the copy? Were any items typed either above or below the line?
- errors in numbers.

Tips for breaking words

- Divide a word into pronounceable parts only (syllables).
- Divide hyphenated words at the hyphen only.
- Divide a word with double consonants between the consonants (e.g. *let-ter*).
- If a word has a prefix or a suffix, divide it after the prefix or before the suffix.

Keep in mind

- Never break a one-syllable word (e.g. *type, mail*).
- Never break a word so that a single letter stands alone.
- Never break names (e.g. *Mrs Johnson, Anthony*).

? Questions

1 Compare the original and the typewritten copy shown below. Look for spelling and punctuation mistakes. Above each line, write the correct spelling of each misspelt word. Add any missing punctuation. Cross out those marks that should not be there. The first line has been done for you.

Original (handwritten):

Within the next twenty years computers that speak will be common in Britain's homes and offices. The public will become accustomed to hearing computer voices when they use the telephone for time, temperature and weather reports. Some overseas business firms already use audio output systems for credit verification and financial calculation. Since technology has progressed to the point where audio responses sound almost natural, a vastly wider market for these computers can be predicted.

Typewritten copy:

next
Within the ~~nezt~~ twenty years,
　　　　　speak
computers that ~~steak~~ will be common
in Britain's homes and offices. The
public will become acccustomed to
hearing computre boices when use the
telephone for time temperature and
weather reports Som overseas business
firms alreddy use qudio output systems
for credit verifacation and financial
caluclations, Since tehnology has
progressed to the point where audio
response sound almost natural; a
vastly wider market for these compuers
can be perdicted,

Word	Break
quarterly	quar-
month	
eighteen-year-old	
sales	
decide	
government	
progress	
letter	
recommendation	
current	
reimbursement	
suggest	
Mr Oakley	

2 You are typing a report. Each of the words on the right ends a line. You must decide whether the word should be broken. If so, where? The line drawn represents your right-hand margin. If the word should not be broken, write 'no' beside it. If it should, use a hyphen and break it as close to the margin as possible. The first one has been done for you.

Secretary

Secretaries need many skills. They must have a general knowledge of all office jobs. They may have to write, type and use the telephone. They may need to know shorthand. Sometimes their duties include fact-finding. Directories such as Yellow Pages provide them with information. They often have to locate information and take decisions concerning it.

The exercises in this section give practice in secretarial skills.

*Read the **Words you need**. Study the information given. Then answer the questions.

Words you need

direct   straight to the person named
display ads   large ads shown in directories, etc.
express   speedy; without delay

I.O.M.   Isle of Man
shorthand   a fast way of writing notes, especially dictation

How to send a parcel by express delivery

- Look in Yellow Pages for delivery services.
- Read through the display ads for detailed information.
- Compare several different ads and decide which one suits you best.
- Phone some of these for comparison of prices and service.
- Decide on one company.

? Questions

1   Look at the display ads above. Which company would you use if you were sending something to France? Why?

2   Inter County deliver goods all over the country in 24/48 hours. Roadrunner have regular services to I.O.M. and London. What questions do you still need to ask before choosing one of these companies?

3 Roadrunner offer 'direct' delivery. Which words of the Inter County ad suggest direct delivery?

4 You phone a delivery company and they quote a price. How will you check that this is a fair price?

5 Part of your job as a secretary is to arrange hotel/motel bookings. Read and compare these display ads from a Yellow Pages directory. Answer each question:

a A meeting room is required for sales representatives. They will fly in and out on the same day. Which number should you call?

b Your boss asks you to arrange accommodation for a conference. She wants a hotel in a relaxing atmosphere. Which number should you call?

c You have to choose a hotel near the city centre. Which hotel would you choose?

d Your boss asks you to find a hotel for two visitors. They would like to have a game of golf after business. Which hotel would you recommend?

e You have chosen a hotel for your boss and her colleagues. The arrangements have been made by telephone. What should you now do to confirm the arrangement?

The Park Hotel·Motel
* convenient mid-city location
* 2 mins from Central Station
* 500 rooms–colour TV–telephone
* 24-hour room service
* near theatres and business district
* free underground parking
* air-conditioned
* heated pool
* gourmet dining at The Trees Restaurant
* all major credit cards accepted
620 Park Crescent
555-1270

TOWER INN
colour TV
restaurant
air-conditioned
heated pool
meeting rooms
convention facilities
all major credit cards accepted

5 MINUTES FROM AIRPORT
666-3715
284-286 Lakeside Drive, Manchester

North-Shore Motor Inn
Northern Parkway, Scarborough 234-1978
* quiet, country atmosphere
* beach
* meeting rooms
* pool and sauna
* tennis courts, golf course
* dining room specialising in seafood
* colour TV

6 Secretaries often have to write letters making or confirming arrangements. They should know how to set out and punctuate a letter. The following letter has a lot of mistakes. Rewrite it correctly on a piece of paper.

manager
the park hotel
620 park crescent
birmingham

tudorgate ltd
13 burtonwood airfield
warrington
14 dec 1984

dear sir
this is to confirm a booking made by telephone on 12 december please reserve two single rooms with bath in the names of mr david jones and mr brian lovelace for the nights of 22 dec and 23 dec 1984 could you please arrange a meeting room for four for 10 am on 23 dec
yours sincerely   paul wright

Revision

1 We have seen how the following words are used in office jobs. Now use the words to complete the sentences on the right.

accuracy
diagram
display ads
hyphen
instructions
margins
original
quantity
shorthand
syllables
transcribe
typing speed
Yellow Pages

2 Write out these abbreviated words in full:

ext. – _____

memo – _____

I.O.M. – _____

Ltd – _____

plc – _____

3 Read the list of files below and number them in alphabetical order:

_____ Anne Newman
_____ H.C. Oysters Ltd
_____ 1-2-3 Driving School
_____ The Nedlands Company Ltd
_____ R.D. Newham
_____ Albert Newman
_____ Richards Bedding

a The _____ of the machine shows its different parts.
b Follow the operating _____.
c You cannot make good copies if the _____ is barely readable.
d To take dictation quickly, it helps if you can write _____.
e A dash between parts of words is called a _____.
f Look for the telephone number of Aer Lingus under 'Air Services' in _____.
g If your company wants to announce its services in the newspapers, it can use _____.
h Make your typed pages look neat and attractive; set your _____.

4 Add a suffix or prefix to the following to make new words:

sense _____

good _____

possible _____

quarter _____

5 Give the meanings of the following words:

chronologically _____

correspondence _____

verify _____

express _____

hyphen _____

duplicate _____

multiple _____

urgent _____

Outdoor SPORTS CENTRE
297 2868
110 Phillip Street, Bedford

- Golf • Soccer • Tennis
- Rugby • Fishing • Surfing
- Scuba-diving • Water-skiing
- Cricket

Large range always in stock. Full repair service available for all sporting gear.

Specialists in Sporting Goods for Outdoor Sports

AQUA SCUBA GEAR Ltd
Custom wet-suits for divers, skiers & surfers
Aqualung sales & service
Diving equipment for hire
37 Collins Rd, Bedford 297 6646

Barrett & Bryce Ltd 371 Murray Rd
.... 297 4630
(See advertisement This Classification)

BIKE WORLD 17A Wilson St ..297 4692
Brett's Golf Supplies 103 Wilson St
.... 297 6666

Burrows' Golf Centre 9 Kingston Ave
.... 297 7363
Central Sports Warehouse 276 Julia St
.... 297 1362

6 You might find display ads like these above in Yellow Pages. Read them carefully and then answer the questions below:

a You want to buy a football. Which shop will have one?

_____

b You want a new ten-speed racing bike. Which telephone number would you ring for information?

_____

c Would you be able to buy a squash racket at 110 Philip Street?

_____

7 Rewrite this business letter on the office stationery on the right. Punctuate.

12 december 1985

ms patricia wagner
22 circle drive
wellington
n. yorks XY1 6ST

dear ms wagner

we are happy to advise you that your interview with us was successful congratulations you have the job and can start at 9 a m next monday if you have any questions please telephone me

yours sincerely

carol collins
personnel manager

Kelsall Nursery
573 Napier Drive, Wellington, North Yorks XY1 6ST

8 Write a file label for each group of items described below:

Group A. Mail to customers; letters from clients; letters to and from other companies.

_____

Group B. Notes to and from people working in the same office; reminders to staff from the manager.

_____

Group C. Wage rates for employees; casual pay rates; holiday pay records.

_____

Group D. Names and addresses of clients in other countries.

_____

9 You are typing a letter. Some words will go over the right-hand margin unless you break them. Use a hyphen to show where these words should be broken:

in February   _____

our products   _____

the delivery   _____

continuously   _____

is operating   _____

10 Suppose that you work in an office. You take the following phone call. Read the dialogue carefully. Then write the telephone message on the form provided. The time is noon and the date is today.

Caller: Hello. Is Mrs Van Doorn in?
You: Yes, but she's with a client at the moment. May I ask who's calling?
Caller: Anne Stevens.
You: Is that A–N–N–E S–T–E–V–E–N–S?
Caller: That's right.
You: May I have your phone number please?
Caller: Yes, it's 522 373 – Dialling code 043.
You: Would you like to leave a message?
Caller: Yes. I'm an old friend of Mrs Van Doorn. We went to school together and we both belong to the Keep Fit Club. I've been overseas for the past year. I'd like to see her soon. Perhaps she'll come over for dinner. Would you ask her to phone me, please?

WHILE YOU WERE OUT

To_____

Date_____ Time_____ a.m./p.m.

M_____

of_____

Phone_____ Ext._____

_____

☐ telephoned   ☐ please call
☐ wanted to see you   ☐ will call again
☐ called to see you   ☐ urgent

Message_____

_____

_____

Operator_____

Unit 4 Social jobs

We call jobs in this unit 'social' because they are all based on contact with people. If you like meeting and helping people, these sorts of jobs may suit you. Where qualifications and training are needed, these are discussed. But all these jobs require you to be pleasant, friendly and helpful. They also require reading and writing skills.

Shop assistant Reading signs and categorising	52
Dry-cleaners shop assistant Using abbreviations	54
Waiter/waitress Reading a menu	56
Nurse: Enrolled Nurse (General) Keeping records and reading charts	58
Cashier (in a shop) Keeping cash records	60
Revision	62

Shop assistant

Reading signs and categorising

Shop assistants must know about the *specific* goods they are selling. People may ask you to help them find an item. You must know the categories into which products are grouped. Shop assistants must know how to read signs and labels. They must also be able to follow and give directions.

The exercises in this section give practice in skills needed by shop assistants. They are: reading signs and labels; categorising; following and giving directions.

*Read the **Words you need**. Study the information on stocking and categorising. Look at the supermarket aisle plan and answer the questions.

Words you need

aisle passage between two rows of shelves
beverages drinks: tea, coffee, etc.
category class or group of things with something in common
condiments seasoning to flavour food, e.g. salt, spices
cosmetics beauty creams, etc.
delicatessen shop selling cooked meats and other prepared foods
item single thing
location place where something can be found
specific of a particular kind
stock goods for sale

Stocking and categorising goods

- In nearly all shops goods are grouped in categories, e.g. hammers, saws and pliers are grouped under TOOLS.
- Items are stocked on shelves on both sides of an aisle.
- In large department stores and supermarkets there may be many aisles. Usually signs are hung above the aisles. These show the categories of goods on the shelves.
- Each aisle has two sides – left and right. But *left* and *right* depend on which way you are facing. When giving customers directions, make sure you both face the same way.
- Remember customers return to shops where assistants are polite and eager to help. When you ask 'May I help you?' follow this up by *being* helpful.

Supermarket Aisle Plan

A	Frozen Foods, Dairy Products

Aisle 1

B	Meat, Delicatessen
A	Fruit and Vegetables

Aisle 2

B	Baking Needs, Bread, Cakes
A	Pasta, Sauces

Aisle 3

B	Beverages, Cereals
A	Tinned Foods, International Foods

Aisle 4

B	Herbs, Spices, Condiments, Sugar
A	Paper Goods, Pet Supplies

Aisle 5

B	Household Supplies, Cleansers

? Questions

1 Study the supermarket aisles on the opposite page. You have to stock the shelves with the items listed below. Write the items on the lines provided by the aisle locations. The first one has been done for you. Cross out the item when you stock it.

   Items to be stocked
   t~~ea~~, cottage cheese, flour, fresh tomatoes, butter, salt, soap, pepper, tinned beetroot, frozen peas, eggs, flea collars, chops, tissues, detergent, scones, tinned soup, cat food, coffee, apples, cornflakes, tomato sauce, sausages, bleach.

   Aisle location
   1A _____
   1B _____
   2A _____
   2B _____
   3A _____
   3B _tea_
   4A _____
   4B _____
   5A _____
   5B _____

2 You work in this chemist shop. The floor plan is shown on the right. Various customers have asked you where they can find certain items. What directions would you give them? Fill in the table below with the correct aisle number and *side* of the aisle. The first one has been done for you.

3 Look at these items: sheets, blankets, pillows. They are grouped in one category – bedding – as they go together. On the lines under the following items write the category name.
   pens, pencils, notepaper:
a _____
   cots, prams, playpens:
b _____
   buttons, cotton, needles:
c _____
   radios, stereos, speakers:
d _____

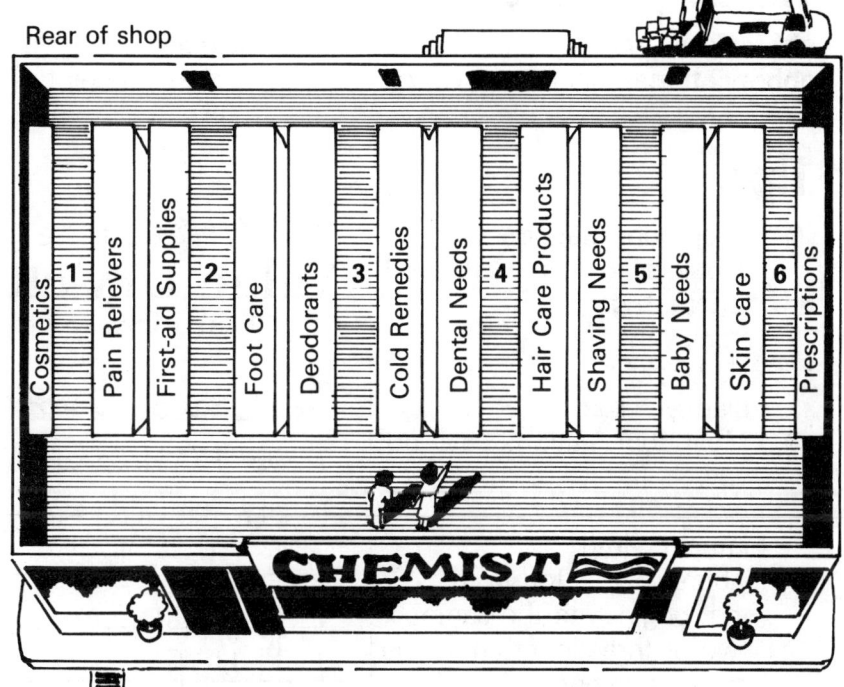

Your location	Product requested	Aisle	Side
aisle 2, front	razor blades	5	left
aisle 6, front	toothpaste		
aisle 2, rear	cough syrup		
aisle 1, front	shampoo		
aisle 1, rear	hand lotion		
aisle 4, front	bandages		

Dry-cleaners shop assistant

Using abbreviations

Filling in dry-cleaning *tickets* is something like writing secret messages. There's a lot of information to put on the ticket, but everything can be in code in abbreviated form. This saves time and space. Study how to *abbreviate* and you can write the dry-cleaners' codes.

*Read the **Words you need**. Study the tips for abbreviating. Look carefully at the tickets. Note how they are completed. Then answer the questions.

Words you need

abbreviate   make words shorter
abbreviations   shortened words
article   item left for dry-cleaning
ticket   receipt given to a customer

Tips

- Keep abbreviations short, if possible, to no more than 4 letters, e.g.
  frock = fr
  skirt = skt
  blanket = blkt
- Most abbreviations have no vowels (a, e, i, o, u):
  jacket = jkt
  jumper = jmpr
- Abbreviations for words that begin with the same two or three letters must be made different:
  blue = bl
  black = blk
  green = gr
  grey = gry

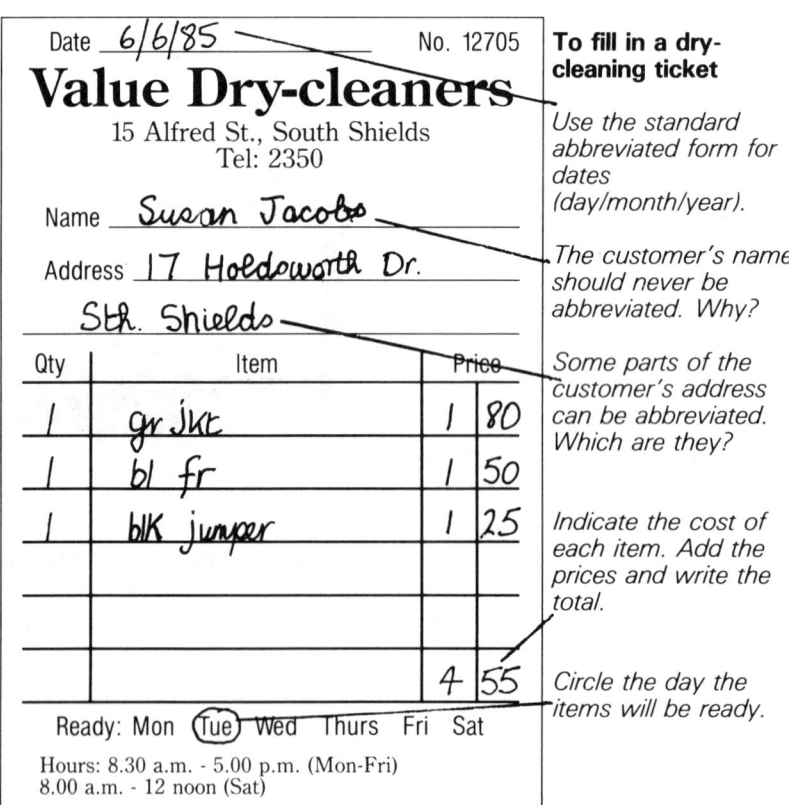

? Questions

1 Make up your own abbreviations for the following words:
a overcoat _____   **d** raincoat _____
b cushion covers _____   **e** candy-striped sheet _____
c orange bedspread _____   **f** cardigan _____

2 Write abbreviations for the following items:

a green curtains

b yellow skirt

c brown slacks

d pink blanket

e red striped frock

f blue and white jumper

g grey checked jacket

3 Fill in the dry-cleaning ticket on the right for the following customer. Use today's date, enter the price of the items from the price chart above, and mark it to show that the articles will be ready in three days.

Terry Phillips of 301 Apple Street, South Shields, brings in a dark-brown suit, a red dress, two pairs of grey trousers and a pair of blue curtains.

4 One customer, Mrs Bertoli, has forgotten to collect her dry-cleaning. Using the ticket copy here, you phone to remind her. List below the articles that the abbreviations stand for.

Price Chart

| Dresses £1.50 | Skirts £1.20 | Jackets £1.80 | Jumpers £1.25 |
| Trousers £1.40 | Suits (Ladies') £2.75 | Suits (Men's) £3.00 | Curtains £5.00 (pr) |

Blankets £2.50

Value Dry-cleaners
15 Alfred St., South Shields
Tel: 2350
No. 12705

Date _____

Name _____
Address _____

Qty	Item	Price

Ready: Mon Tue Wed Thurs Fri Sat
Hours: 8.30 a.m. - 5.00 p.m. (Mon-Fri)
8.00 a.m. - 12 noon (Sat)

Value Dry-cleaners
15 Alfred St., South Shields
Tel: 2350
No. 12705

Name: Mrs R. Bertoli
Address: 21 Rees Rd.
Sth. Shields

Qty	Item	Price	
2	pr pk crtns	10	00
1	bl & grey jumpr	1	25
1	y ottr dr	1	50
1	pr bl trs	1	40
1	ldts suit (2 pc)	2	75
		16	90

Ready: Mon (Tue) Wed Thurs Fri Sat
Hours: 8.30 a.m. - 5.00 p.m. (Mon-Fri)
8.00 a.m. - 12 noon (Sat)

Keep in mind
Remember that someone else may have to read your abbreviations. Write out in full any words that you cannot easily abbreviate.

Waiter/waitress

There is a large turnover of staff in the catering business. You often read ads for waiters/waitresses, especially in the summer months. You might be interested in this work, perhaps as a part-timer. You could be on your feet for long hours and you may find it tiring work. You need to be alert and neat, and it pays to have a good memory. You have to be patient and must be respectful to customers, even to those who may be awkward. Customers often look to the waiter/waitress for help in choosing their meals. You should be able to read the menu and explain it.

This section gives practice in reading names and other connected skills.

*Read the **Words you need** carefully. Study the menus below. Then see if you can answer the questions.

Words you need

à la carte menu where items are individually priced
appetiser small portion of food served before the entrée
bolognaise with a meat sauce
chicken Maryland deep-fried, crumbed chicken
consommé clear soup made from meat
entrée dish served before the main course
filet mignon round beef fillet wrapped in bacon
frite fried
garni decorated with bits of food
hors d'oeuvres starters, appetisers
lasagne pasta with meat and cheese
scampi large prawns
table d'hôte menu with a fixed number of courses at a fixed price

---

La Barbacoa Restaurant
A la carte Menu

Hors d'oeuvres				**Soups**	
Chilled Melon	90p			Soup of the Day	45p
Prawn Cocktail	£1.20			Consommé	45p
Avocado Pear	£1.20			Lobster Soup	85p

Pasta & Seafood	*Entrée*	*Main Course*	**Specialities**	
Spaghetti Bolognaise	£2.60	£4.75	Grilled Sirloin Steak	£6.30
Lasagne	£2.80	£4.90	Filet Mignon	£6.85
King Prawns in Wine	£4.20	£8.30	Chicken Maryland	£5.35
Scampi Frite	£2.95	£5.00	Lamb Cutlets Garni	£4.95

Vegetables: Garden Peas; French Beans; Fried Onions   35p
Broccoli; Mushrooms; Cauliflower   45p
Asparagus Tips   60p

Desserts (All at £1.20): Fresh Fruit & Ice Cream; Gateau; Cheesecake; Cheeses (selection).
Coffee or Tea   45p

La Barbacoa Restaurant
Table d'Hôte Menu – £5.50

Starters
Soup of the Day
Fresh Melon
Spaghetti Bolognaise

Main Course
Rainbow Trout
Roast Beef &
Yorkshire Pudding
Roast Lamb

Sweets
Apple Pie & Custard
Fruit & Ice Cream
Cheeseboard

Beverages
Tea
or
Coffee

Choice of vegetables with main course: Potatoes (roast, baked or chipped) with cauliflower, peas, or carrots. A 10% service charge is added.

? Questions

1 Look at the two menus. Write down here all the French words you can find:
   _____
   _____
   _____

2 10% service charge means 10p in every pound. How much service charge would you pay if your meal costs
   a £5.50? _____
   b £8.00? _____
   c £11.50? _____

3 In some restaurants the waiters may have to write out menus. The following foods are jumbled up. Put them on the lines next to their heading:
   Roast Rib of Beef; Turtle Soup; Scampi Frite; Sherry Trifle; Roast Duckling; Consommé; Apple Pie; Avocado Pear.
   HORS D'OEUVRE _____
   SOUP _____
   _____
   MAIN COURSE _____
   _____
   _____
   SWEET _____
   _____

4 A customer ordered the meal listed here. Write the cost next to each item and total the amount.
   Hors d'oeuvres
   Prawn Cocktail   _____
   Entrée
   Lasagne   _____
   Main Course
   Filet Mignon   _____
   Vegetables
   Asparagus Tips   _____
   Sweet
   Gateau   _____
   Coffee   _____
   TOTAL   _____

5 Two friends have a meal in the restaurant. He orders the table d'hôte menu. She orders consommé, sirloin steak with fried onions, gateau and coffee. Which meal is more expensive? By how much? _____
   _____
   _____

6 What advantage has the à la carte meal over the table d'hôte?
   _____
   _____

Nurse: Enrolled Nurse (General) (E.N.(G))

Keeping records and reading charts

Nurses must do a two or three year training course. Their training takes place mainly in a hospital school of nursing. The hospital schools often demand 'O' levels. However, there are nursing cadet schemes in some areas and also pre-nursing courses in some Colleges. These may simply ask for CSEs in maths and English. Some schemes rely on their own entrance tests. Nursing cadet schemes may be started at 16 or 17. Nurses need to learn about hygiene, medicine and illness. They must be able to keep records and write reports.

This section is concerned with recording temperature, pulse and breathing. It gives practice in reading the charts related to them.

*Read the **Words you need** carefully. Read the information on temperature, pulse and respiration. Study the chart. Then see if you can answer the questions.

Words you need

admission entrance
centigrade a temperature scale of 100 degrees
Celcius the man who invented the centigrade thermometer
discharged released
expelled forced out

expiration breathing out
Fahrenheit temperature scale with freezing point at 32 and boiling point at 212 degrees
inspiration breathing in
respiration breathing
variations alterations, differences

Temperature (F = Fahrenheit; C = Centigrade or Celcius)

A patient's temperature is taken with a thermometer. The body temperature of a healthy person ranges between 97 and 99F (36 to 37.2C). The average temperature in health is 98.4F (36.9C). It also varies at different times of the day. It may rise to one degree higher in the evening. Temperatures should be taken when the patient is sitting or lying down. They should not be taken after a hot bath or hot drink.

Pulse (Average for an adult: 72 beats per minute)

This is an important guide to the condition of the patient. It is felt in an artery as blood pumps through from the heart. The pulse is felt as the artery expands.

Variations in the pulse rate
Infants: 140 beats per minute. At 12 months of age: 120 beats per minute.
Children: 100–90 beats per minute.
Adults: 80–60 beats per minute.
Exercise, drugs, disease and emotions all affect the pulse rate.

Respiration (Normal adult breathing rate is 16 to 24 times per minute)

During inspiration oxygen passes through the lungs into the blood. During expiration carbon dioxide from the blood is expelled from the lungs. Any interference with breathing causes the body to be deprived of oxygen. The patient will then show signs of distress. Respiration rate should be counted when the patient is at rest and without his or her knowledge. This avoids any conscious change in the rate of breathing.

? Questions (Look at the chart on the right)

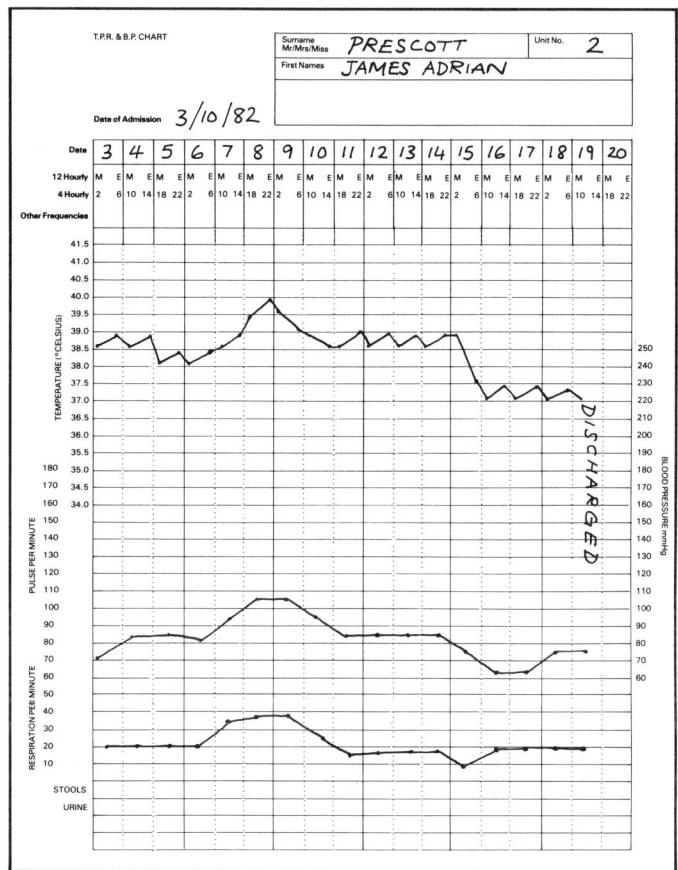

1. What are the normal rates for an adult?
   pulse rate _____
   respiration _____
   temperature _____

2. What things can alter a person's pulse rate?
   _____
   _____

3. On the TPR chart what was the patient's temperature _____;
   pulse _____; respiration _____
   on admission?

4. On what date was respiration at its lowest?
   _____

5. When is a person's temperature likely to be higher, morning or evening?
   _____

6. On what date was the patient discharged?
   _____

7. On what day did the patient reach a crisis in his illness?
   _____

Cashier (in a shop)

Keeping cash records

Shop assistants may have to serve and handle cash. Sometimes one person works only at the cash register. Cashiers in supermarkets, for instance, handle cash (coins and notes) and cheques. They must be accurate. There are all sorts of cash registers and cash records. However, the skills needed are similar for all of them. Cashiers in shops may have to keep written records, though this is often done by a supervisor. This section is about handling cash and records in a shop.

*Read the **Words you need**. Do you know them? Study the tips for filling in a cash balance form. Then answer the questions.

Words you need

balance the result when you take one amount of money from another
denom. (denomination) the value of a single note or coin
drawer person whose signature is on a cheque
float money in the till at the beginning of each shift
shift a set period of working time
tape a printed record of amounts rung up on a cash register
void invalid; amount rung up by mistake

How to fill in a cash balance form

A Count the notes in the till. Write the value of each in the *Denom.* column. Write the number of each in the *No.* column. Multiply the number by the value. Write the amount in the *Total* column. Do the same with the coins.

B Write the details for each cheque and add up the amounts.

C Add the totals for both notes and coins.

D Add the totals of cheques, notes and coins to give *Total Cash*.

E Write the value of your float. Add this to the total of your voids for the day. This gives *Total Out*.

F *Total Cash* less *Total Out* gives the *Balance*.

G Write the amount printed on your cash register tape.

H Compare your balance with the printed amount on the cash register tape. Is it over or under?

CASH BALANCE FORM

Date _____ Operator No. _____ Shift _____ to _____ Register No. _____

NOTES			COINS			CHEQUES		
Denom.	No.	Total	Denom.	No.	Total	Drawer	Bank	Amt.
£20 £10 £5 £1	3	60	50p 20p 10p 5p 2p 1p			P. Leeman	GIRO	56.00
TOTAL NOTES			**TOTAL COINS**			**TOTAL CHEQUES**		

Float _____
Voids _____
TOTAL OUT _____

TOTAL NOTES _____
TOTAL COINS _____
TOTAL CASH _____
Less TOTAL OUT _____
BALANCE _____
TAPE _____
Amount Over _____
Amount Under _____

? Questions

1a Suppose that you work in a department store on the 1 p.m. to 9 p.m. shift. Fill in the cash balance form on page 60. Use today's date. Your operator number is 19. You have been on cash register No. 3 with a float of £150. You have the following cash in the till: 3 × £20; 19 × £10; 15 × £5; 12 × £1; 50 × 50p; 30 × 20p; 70 × 10p; 50 × 5p; 60 × 2p and 45 × 1p.
There are two cheques: one drawn by Peter Leeman on the Giro Bank for £56.00, and one on Barclays by Angela Brown for £25.50. You have voids totalling £9.10. Your tape shows £298.65.

b If your cash is 'over', what might have happened? Tick all possible answers below.
- [ ] You gave someone too much change
- [ ] You gave someone too little change
- [ ] You rang up too much on the cash register
- [ ] You rang up too little on the cash register.

c If your cash is 'under', what might have happened? Tick all possible answers below.
- [ ] You rang up too much on the cash register
- [ ] You rang up too little on the cash register
- [ ] You gave someone too much change
- [ ] You gave someone too little change.

d Was your total 'over' or 'under'? Or was it correct? If not correct, say by how much.

2 A customer thinks she has been overcharged. You will have to add up the price of the items in your head. Can you work out what these cost?

Coffee	89p
Bread	39p
Sugar	37p
Tea	42p
Butter	<u>84p</u>
TOTAL	____

3 You ring up £1.20 for an item instead of 80p. The customer's next item costs 60p. How can you put this right?

Revision

1 Read this supermarket sign and answer the questions.

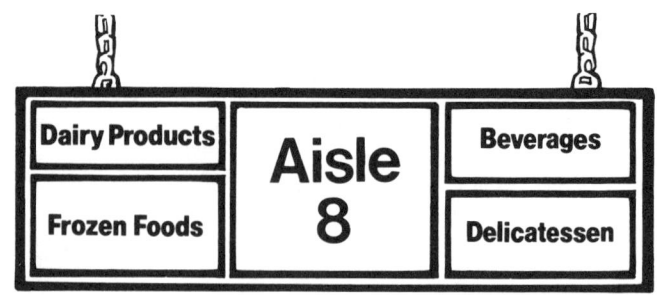

a You are directly in front of the sign when the customer asks you where the fresh cream is. Should you point to the left or to the right?

b On which side should hot cooked chickens be found?

2 A customer is at the checkout with some items that are currently reduced. Use the chart to add up his purchases correctly. What would the total be?

3 Read these labels. Which product would you recommend for the customers below? Write the product's name in the blank provided.

a Jeanette's car has a few rusty spots. Which polish does she need?

b Alexis wants to polish his car without working too hard. Which polish should he use?

4 Can you complete these sentences?

a Green beans, tomatoes and carrots may be grouped in the same _____.

b A small portion of food served before the entrée is an _____.

c The money in a cash register at the start of each shift is called a _____.

d The goods for sale in a shop are the _____.

e The difference between two amounts of money is called the _____.

f You have been ill in hospital. Now you are better, you will be _____.

g To get articles back from the dry-cleaners, you must present your _____.

h A person who works from 1 p.m. to 7 p.m. is on the afternoon _____.

5 What is the difference between a fahrenheit and a centigrade thermometer?

6 You may see the following words on a menu. What do they mean?

a bolognaise _____

b lasagne _____

c entrée _____

7 The following abbreviations are used in this unit. Do you know what they mean? Write the answers on the lines provided.

a blk. _____

b jkt. _____

c pr. _____

d E.N.(G) _____

e denom. _____

f T.P.R. _____

g No. _____

8 We should not tell a patient that we are checking breathing rate. Why?

9 You give a patient some exciting news. Then you take their pulse rate. What is likely to happen and why?

10 In this unit we have listed a number of 'social' jobs. How many more can you think of? Write as many as you can on these lines:

63

11 Fill in this dry-cleaning ticket for Sophie Chung who lives at 30 Julia Street, South Shields. She brought in a brown skirt, a pair of green corduroy jeans and a tan woollen blazer. The charge for cleaning each item is £1.25. She would like the blazer moth-proofed, and this is £1.00 extra. Put today's date on the ticket. Indicate that the articles will be ready in two days.

12 Look at the menu on page 56.
A customer orders prawn cocktail, lamb cutlets garni, peas, asparagus tips, cheesecake and tea. Write out the bill on the right.

Unit 5 Practical jobs

Some people seem to have a knack for fixing things, making things and putting things together. This unit looks at some jobs that need these skills. Some of these jobs require training, either 'on the job' or through an apprenticeship. If you take up a job like this, some of these skills may be helpful to you. Even if you don't, they will help you to do simple repairs.

Assembly worker   66
Following a diagram and written instructions

Carpenter   68
Following correct procedure

Plumber   70
Identifying problems

Electrician   72
Tracing faults

Motor mechanic   74
Reading flow charts

Revision   76

Assembly worker

Assembly workers usually work in factories. Assemblers make up goods or put together parts of goods. They may have to follow written *instructions* and diagrams. Sometimes they may have to fix things together with glue or nails. They may have to use *soldering* or *welding* equipment. Often they will use machines or special tools. Other assemblers may test and check the finished *products*.

The exercises in this section will make you think about assembly work.

*Read the **Words you need** and the information about assembly work. Then answer the questions.

Words you need

assembly putting things together
instructions explanations; words that tell you how
products things that have been produced, made, or put together

soldering joining metal or wires with melted metal
welding joining metals or plastic by pressing together when softened by heat

Information

A. What do you need?
Assemblers should have good eyesight. Assembly workers usually need nimble fingers. They have to be good at working with their hands. Assemblers should also be good at following instructions. Sometimes these may be written or drawn.

B. What training do you need?
Usually training is given on the job. There may be a special trainer. Often an experienced assembler or the chargehand does the training. The course of training may last a few days only. If the job is more skilful, it may last two or three weeks. Sometimes this may take place in the firm's training school.

C. Is it for me?
Are you a practical person? Assemblers should like making things and putting things together. They should like making things neat and exact. An assembly worker should be a quick worker. Assembly workers usually have to work with other people. They should be able to get on with workmates.

? Questions

1 Three things are named as being needed by an assembly worker. What are they?

2 There may be a special trainer in a factory. Who might this person be?

_____ or _____

3 What type of person is suited to assembly work? The information at C above mentions several qualities. Name them:

Following a diagram and written instructions
MAKING A STUFFED RABBIT

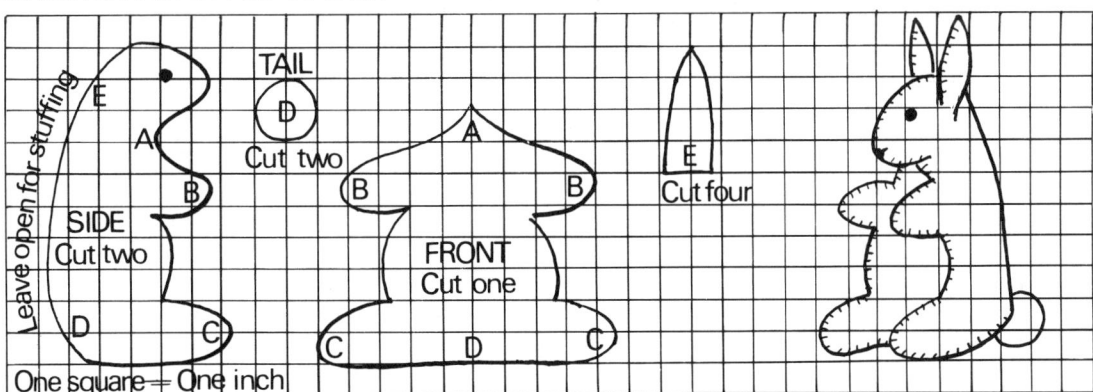

1. Cut out patterns of the right size from card.
2. Lay each pattern over felt and draw round it. (Turn pattern over for the second half of a pair.)
3. Cut out each shape.
4. With right sides together sew body sides and front with stab stitches.
5. Leave an opening for the stuffing.
6. Turn inside out so that seams are inside.
7. Stuff body firmly with kapok.
8. Close up the gap with neat stitches.
9. Make up ears and tail and attach to body with slip stitches.
10. Draw on eyes with pen or sew with coloured thread.

Look at the diagram and instructions above. Can you follow them? An assembler would have to. See if you can answer these questions:

4 Letter D in the diagram shows where the tail goes. What does letter C show?

5 The rabbit must have two sides. What must you do with the pattern to get this?

6 What part of the rabbit is shown by letter B?

7 Why does instruction number 6 tell you to turn the material inside out?

8 How many shapes like E (ears) would you cut out?

9 The rabbit's eyes could be glass or buttons. Why might this *not* be a good idea?

10 Many assembly workers are on piecework. Why would they want to work quickly?

11 Stitches are used to join material together. Put these items with the things that join them:
staples; screws; solder; weld; paste.
 a plastic _____
 b paper _____
 c wires _____
 d cardboard _____
 e wood _____

12 Which of these assembly jobs might be trickiest? Why do you think so?
 a Assembling furniture.
 b Assembling packing cases.
 c Sewing soft toys.
 d Wiring radios.

13 Which would you prefer:
 a to assemble a complete product
 b to make part of a product?
 Say why:

Carpenter

A carpenter used to train as an *apprentice*. Nowadays many start training in the YTS. If you like working outdoors and with wood, this job may suit you. Carpenters need to know about the quality of woods. They have to know how to cut, shape and join wood. An apprentice learns about materials and what tools to use. He or she has to plan out a job in detail.

The exercises in this section are about some of the skills needed by carpenters.

*Read the **Words you need**. Read the information sections. Then answer the questions.

Words you need

apprentice person learning a skilled trade
brads nails with a thin, flat head
dovetail a joint spread out like a dove's tail

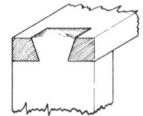

gauge measure
housing recess; space cut out to take hinges, etc.
pare cut away gradually
protrude stick out; project
seasoned matured; grown fit for use
stile upright sidepiece of a door
tenon ends ends of the tenon joint

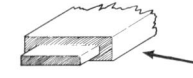

Information on common faults with doors

When wood has not been properly seasoned, it may shrink. This would make a door difficult to open and shut properly. Shrinkage may cause the tenon ends to jut out. The ends that protrude can be planed off. There is no need to take the door off its hinges. Before planing, wedge the door to keep it rigid and steady.

Information on hanging a door

(Requirements – butt hinges, chisel, tenon saw, marking gauge)

1 Gauge the thickness of the hinge. This gives the depth of the housing for the door stile.
2 Measure the depth of the recess by gauging the width of the hinge. Gauge from the centre of the barrel pin to the outside of the flange.
3 Mark the door with the gauge lines. The hinges should be 15cm from the top and bottom of the door.
4 Cut the housing with a tenon saw and pare with a chisel.
5 Screw the hinges in position with the top and bottom screws only.
6 Fit flap and screw heads flush with the door edge.
7 Cut the housing on the inside edge of the frame. Use the marking gauge set to the same measurements as before.
8 Resting the door on wedges, screw in the centre screws lightly.
9 Adjust top and bottom hinges as necessary until door swings perfectly.

Note: If the doors are close to thick carpet, fit rising butt hinges. These have a knuckle joint which lifts the door on opening.

? Questions

1. What may happen to wood if it is not seasoned?

2. Write out the correct sentence:
   Tenon ends may protrude through shrinkage.
   Tenon ends may preclude through shrinkage.

3. What are you told to mark the door with?

4. Do you cut out the housing on the door or on the frame first?

5. Give another word for 'housing':

6. Put names to these hinges.

   butt hinge   rising butt hinge

   a
   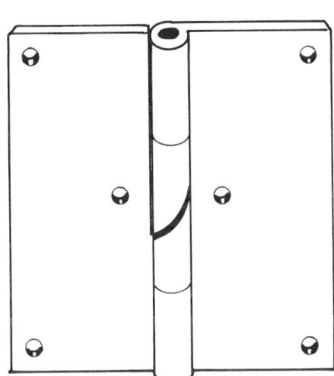

   b
   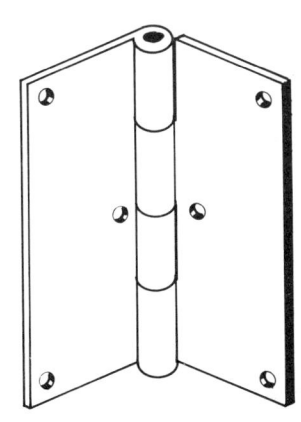

7. How far are the hinges from the top and bottom of the door?

8. What should you do if the door swells?

9. Look at these drawings. Find out the names of the nails. Put the names of the nails by their drawings:

   floor nail   chair nail
   panel pin   lost-head nail

   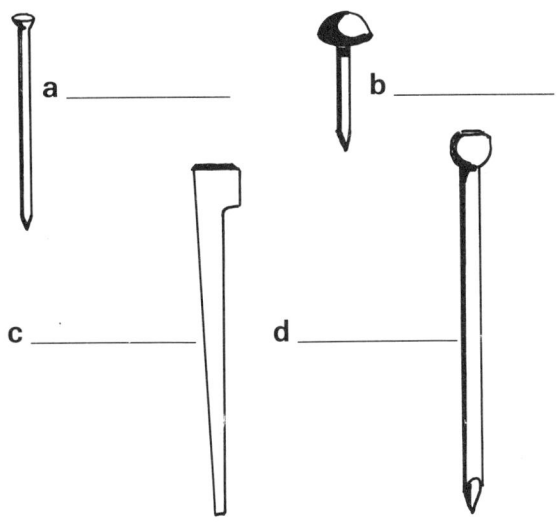

   a _____   b _____
   c _____   d _____

10. Find the sentence from the information on door hanging that goes with the drawing below. Write it here:

    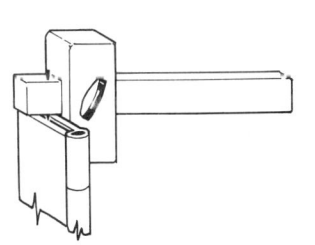

11. Find the sentences from the information on door hanging that go with the drawing below. Write them here:

    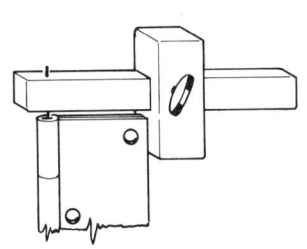

12. Find out the difference between tenon and dovetail joints. Draw one of each type:

Plumber

A plumber will usually have *served an apprenticeship*. Some may train through YTS. He/she has to learn how to use the tools of the trade. There are many skills to learn. One skill is following directions, another is to identify a problem quickly. Once the problem is identified, they must work *systematically* to *rectify* it.

The following exercises give practice in using some skills needed by plumbers.

*Read the **Words you need**. Learn their meanings. Read the information sections and look carefully at the diagrams. Answer the questions for each section as you go.

Words you need

cistern tank for holding water
cotter pin pin for fastening two pieces of metal together
disassemble take apart
main large pipe carrying water
reassemble put together again
rectify put right
served an apprenticeship been an apprentice (for four years as a plumber)

stop-cock valve in a pipe that shuts off and lets in water
systematically orderly, done in order, methodically
washer flat ring of rubber, metal, leather or plastic used to make a waterproof seal

Information on dripping taps

Dripping taps are the most common plumbing problem. Normally a new washer is all that is required. If the tap is connected to the main, turn off the stop-cock. If connected to the cistern, empty this by turning on all taps. If the cistern has a stop-cock, it need not be emptied. Now disassemble the tap.

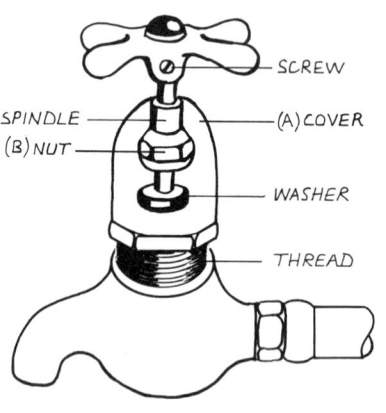

1. Undo the screw on the handle.
2. Now unscrew the cover (A).
3. Undo the large nut (B). It may have a left-hand thread. If so, give it a clockwise turn.
4. The working parts of the tap should be removed.
5. The washer is at the bottom of the spindle. It is fixed in by a nut or screw.
6. Take off the old washer.
7. Replace with a new one of the same size.
8. Reassemble the tap.

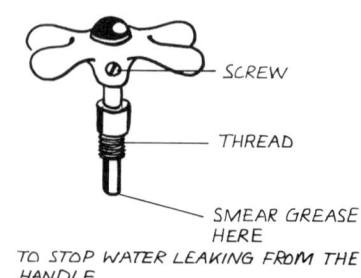
TO STOP WATER LEAKING FROM THE HANDLE

? Questions

1 If a tap drips, what is probably needed? _____
2 What must you do before you disassemble a tap? _____
3 How is a washer attached to the spindle? _____
4 Your tap is connected to the cistern. Where should you turn off the water? _____
5 Where is the main stop-cock in your house? _____
6 You find the new washer is smaller than the old one. What do you think will happen if you fit it? _____
7 Before draining the taps you should switch off the immersion heater. Why? _____
8 The tap leaks from the handle. Write down here what you must do:
   i Turn off _____
   ii _____
   iii _____
   iv _____
   v _____
   vi _____

Information on cisterns

Sometimes water may drip from the overflow pipe. There could be two causes: a) the valve may not be working properly; b) the ball may be waterlogged. If this trouble is not rectified, the drip may become a flood!

The cistern is usually found in the loft. The valve is at the end of the inlet water pipe in the tank. The ball floats on the surface of the water. When the water level is high there should be no flow of water. If water flows the valve must be removed and a new washer fitted. First, turn off the water at the stop-cock. Now disassemble the arm and ball:

1 Remove the small cotter pin. This may have to be tapped out.
2 At the same time this will release the arm and plug. Put a hand under the valve to catch the plug.
3 Unscrew the lower section of the plug.
4 Remove the old washer.
5 Replace with a new washer of the same size.
6 Reassemble.

Note: Shake the ball to see if it is waterlogged. A metal ball can be soldered. It might be easier to replace a plastic ball if it leaks.

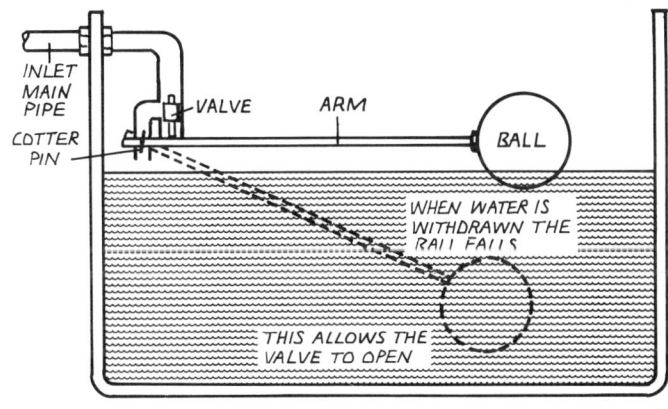

9 What might happen if a cistern had no overflow pipe? _____
10 Which tools would you need to fix the overflow? _____
11 How will you know if the ball is waterlogged? _____
12 What happens if the ball does not float? _____

Electrician

Electricians usually serve an apprenticeship, or training can start in YTS. An apprentice must learn many skills, about wiring, *fuses* and switches, how to trace faults in electrical systems, and how to repair and replace *appliances*.

The exercises on these pages are about some of the skills used by electricians.

*Read the **Words you need** carefully. Study the skills information. Then answer the questions.

Words you need

appliance   electrical equipment
ceiling rose   cover where the lighting flex comes through the ceiling
circuit   path taken by electric current
elimination   ruling out step by step
flex   insulated wire

fuse   thin piece of wire acting as a safeguard
porcelain   white, glazed china
terminal   metal attachment, e.g. screws at the end of a circuit

Information

Safety warning: Do not touch bare wires and terminals when power is ON.

Making a pilot lamp (Testing lamp – used for tracing faults)

Get an ordinary lamp holder. Fit this with a 40 watt lamp. Connect with a 1.2m length of flex. The ends of the flex should be bared ready for each connection. Special clips called 'crocodile clips' can be attached to the ends. These grip the terminals tightly.

Tracing a fault (e.g. a ceiling lamp fails to light)

Proceed by a process of elimination.
1 Switch on all other lamps in the circuit. If they light, the ceiling bulb has gone.
2 If the other lamps fail to light: the trouble will probably be a blown fuse.
3 If the fuse is all right: the fault may be in the switch.
4 In that case unscrew the cover piece of the switch. Connect the flex endings of a pilot lamp to the switch terminals. Put the switch ON. The pilot lamp and suspected faulty lamp should light up dimly.
5 If the lamps do not light: use the pilot lamp on the ceiling rose. Put the switch ON. If the lamp lights, the fault is in one of two places: the ceiling flex or the lamp holder.

Replacing a blown fuse in the power and lighting circuit

1 Switch off the current at the main.
2 Undo the door of the fuse box.
3 Take out and examine each fuse carrier. The blown fuse will have broken wire and be burnt.

4 Undo the two screws holding the broken ends of the wire.
5 Remove the broken wire. Wipe away any carbon on the porcelain top of the carrier.
6 Fit a new length of fuse wire of the correct grade.
7 Tighten up the screws and cut off the ends of the wire.
8 Put the carrier back in place and shut the fuse box.
9 Switch on the current at the main switch.

Note: The main grades of fuse wire –   5 amp. – lighting
                                        15 amp. – heating
                                        30 amp. – power

? Questions

1 If all the lamps in one circuit fail, what could the fault be?

2 All the lamps but one in a circuit light. What could the fault be?

3 How would you test that a light switch is working properly?

4 Tracing faults is done by a process of elimination. The process of tracing a fault has been jumbled up here. Put these items in the correct order:

   faulty switch   a _____
   ceiling flex   b _____
   broken lamp   c _____
   lamp holder   d _____
   blown fuse   e _____

5 What is a pilot lamp used for?

6 What do we call the special clips for gripping terminals?

7 What is the first thing to do when replacing a fuse?

8 If a blown fuse has thin fuse wire (5 amp.), should it be replaced with thick (30 amp.) wire? Can you give reasons?

9 What type of fuse wire is used for heating?

10 How can you recognise a blown fuse when you see it?

11 Why do we use fuses?

12 Write down the names of six electrical appliances used in the home:

13 Below are drawings of two fuse carriers. One fuse has blown. Label the drawings with these words:

fuse wire
porcelain top
carbon
screw terminal
broken wire

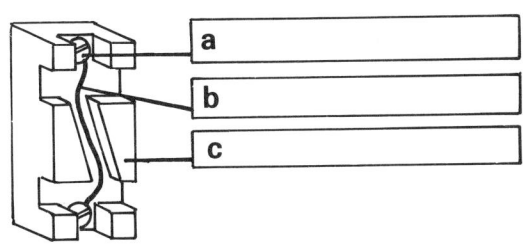

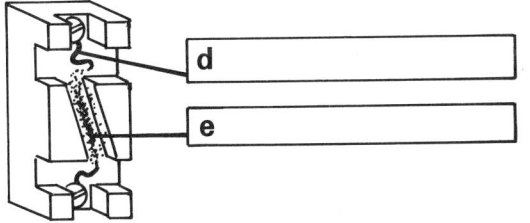

Motor mechanic

Reading flow charts

Motor mechanics, like most workers in this unit, often receive apprenticeship training. Every car owner has problems sometimes. Perhaps you can do simple repairs already. This is a good start, but only a start. As a motor mechanic you must deal with all kinds of cars. You must deal with problems quickly and *efficiently*. Motor mechanics often refer to special car-repair manuals. One of the most helpful types of chart is a *flow chart*. It helps you to solve a problem without guessing and wasting time.

This section helps you to learn how to follow a flow chart.

*Read the **Words you need**. Do you know them? Study the flow chart. Then answer the questions.

Words you need

diagnose work out the cause of a problem

efficiently using the least time and effort possible

mechanic a person who services and repairs machines

outcome the result of doing something

Tips

- Notice that each step is written in a box.
- Read the chart from top to bottom. Your investigation 'flows' from top to bottom. Each move depends upon the outcome of each step you take.
- Some charts have only a few steps. Others can be long and complicated. But their purpose is always the same: to diagnose the cause of the problem quickly.

This is part of a flow chart

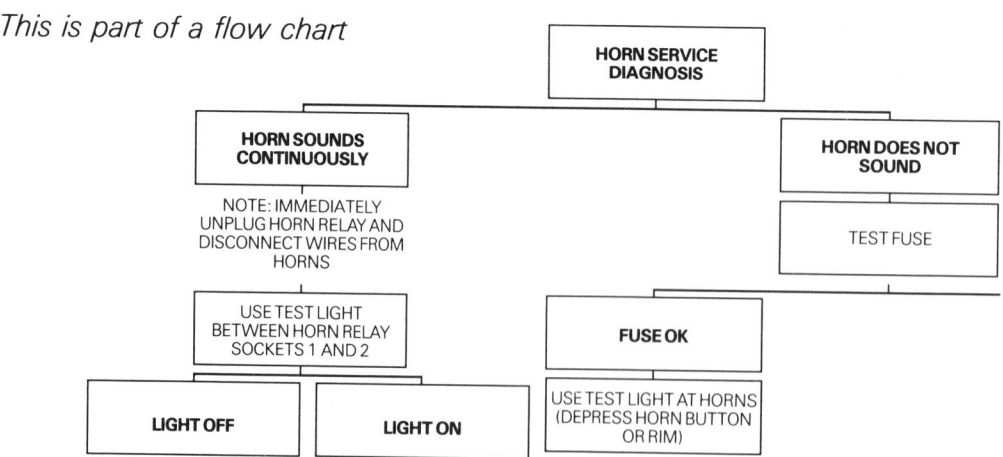

According to the horn service chart above:
- A faulty horn doesn't sound at all or it sounds continuously.
- If you follow the direction of the chart from this box, the next box will tell you what to do.
- The following boxes will give you the possible outcomes.

```
HORN DOES
NOT SOUND

OPEN CIRCUIT IN WIRE
BETWEEN HORN RELAY
SOCKETS AND HORNS
```

Study the complete flow chart for diagnosing the service of a car horn.

```
                              HORN SERVICE
                              DIAGNOSIS
              ┌───────────────────┴───────────────────┐
       HORN SOUNDS                              HORN DOES NOT
       CONTINUOUSLY                             SOUND
                                                     │
       NOTE: IMMEDIATELY                        TEST FUSE
       UNPLUG HORN RELAY AND
       DISCONNECT WIRES FROM               ┌────────┴────────┐
       HORNS.                           FUSE OK          FUSE BLOWN
       USE TEST LIGHT
       BETWEEN HORN RELAY            USE TEST LIGHT AT HORNS    HORN CIRCUIT WIRING
       SOCKETS 1 AND 2               (DEPRESS HORN BUTTON        SHORTED TO EARTH
                                      OR RIM)
   ┌───────┴───────┐            ┌────────┴────────┐           HORN SHORTED TO
 LIGHT OFF     LIGHT ON       LIGHT OFF        LIGHT ON        EARTH

 FAULTY HORN   WIRE TO HORN   DEPRESS HORN     HORN NOT        SHORTED HORN RELAY
 RELAY         BUTTON SWITCH  BUTTON OR RIM    EARTHED
               EARTHED, OR    AND LISTEN FOR
               HORN BUTTON    AUDIBLE CLICK    FAULTY HORN     SHORT BETWEEN HORN
               SWITCH         AT HORN RELAY    ADJUSTMENT      RELAY SOCKET AND
               EARTHED                                         EARTH
                              HORN RELAY       FAULTY HORN
                              CLICKS

                              LOOSE FUSE BLOCK
                              BULKHEAD CONNECTOR

                              OPEN CIRCUIT IN WIRE
                              FROM RELAY TO HORNS       HORN RELAY DOES NOT
                                                        CLICK
                              FAULTY RELAY
                                                        REMOVE HORN RELAY
                                                        FROM SOCKET, TOUCH
                                                        JUMPER WIRE BETWEEN
                                                        RELAY SOCKETS 1 AND 3

                              HORN DOES          HORN SOUNDS
                              NOT SOUND

                              OPEN CIRCUIT IN WIRE   PLACE JUMPER WIRE
                              BETWEEN HORN RELAY     BETWEEN HORN RELAY
                              SOCKETS AND HORNS      SOCKETS 1 AND 2, DEPRESS
                                                     HORN BUTTON OR RIM
                              FAULTY RELAY SOCKET
                              CONNECTION         ┌──────────┴──────────┐
                                              HORN DOES            HORN SOUNDS
                                              NOT SOUND

                                              FAULTY HORN BUTTON   FAULTY HORN RELAY
                                              SWITCH CONNECTIONS
                                              OR WIRING
```

? Questions

1 With the help of the flow chart, circle each word or phrase that answers the question correctly.

a In which direction should this flow chart be followed?
 left to right
 bottom to top
 right to left
 top to bottom

b What is given in the boxes with darker letters?
 warnings
 directions
 possible outcomes

c According to the chart, what is the first thing to do if the horn does not sound?
 Test fuse.
 Use test light.
 Push horn button.

d How many things might have caused a blown fuse?
 two
 four
 six

2 Write your answers to the following question on the lines provided.
Mr Milton's car horn does not sound at all. You checked the fuse and it was all right. You used the test light and it stayed on. What are the three possible causes of Mr Milton's problem?

a _____

b _____

c _____

75

Revision

1 Synonyms are words that have the same meaning. Circle the synonyms for the words underlined.

a Assemblers put <u>manufactured goods</u> together.
  parts   products   pieces

b The mechanic said he would have to <u>work out</u> the cause of the problem.
  repair   contrast   diagnose

c A flow chart helps you to work <u>with the least time and effort</u>.
  correctly   efficiently   slowly

d A piece of wood was <u>sticking out</u> of the doorway.
  protruding   rising   housing

e There are many electrical <u>appliances</u> in the kitchen.
  outlets   machines   engines

2 Antonyms are words that have the opposite meaning. Circle the antonym for the first word in each line below.

a assemble	examine	investigate	disassemble
b relevant	similar	irrelevant	different
c cause	reason	meaning	effect
d problem	effect	solution	diagnosis
e part	main	valve	whole

3 Prefixes and suffixes are clues to the meanings of words. Study each underlined prefix or suffix. Then complete the meaning of the word.

a <u>re</u>assemble: put together _____

b repair<u>er</u>: _____ fixes things

c <u>un</u>finished: _____ complete

d cause<u>less</u>: _____ a cause

4 The following words are spelt incorrectly. Correct them.

diegnose _____
soldaring _____
produkts _____
aprentice _____
sircuit _____
instrucktions _____
probblem _____
removeing _____
meckanic _____
sollution _____

5 Use *one* word instead of those underlined

a <u>put right</u> – _____

b <u>put together</u> – _____

c <u>path taken by electricity</u> – _____

d <u>join metals by pressing together when heated</u> – _____

6 Read this illustrated set of directions on how to use a hammer. Answer the questions below with complete sentences.

HOW TO USE A CLAW HAMMER

- Hold the hammer near the end of the handle for more hitting power. First, hold a nail in place and tap it gently with the hammer head until it is firmly set. Then hit the nail straight in. (See Fig. 1)

- Use a nail punch (Fig. 2) to avoid hammer marks on the wood. You can also use another nail to drive the nail the last 3 mm into the wood.

- Use the claw end of the hammer to remove a nail. To avoid marking the wood, place a small block of wood under the hammer head. (Fig. 3)

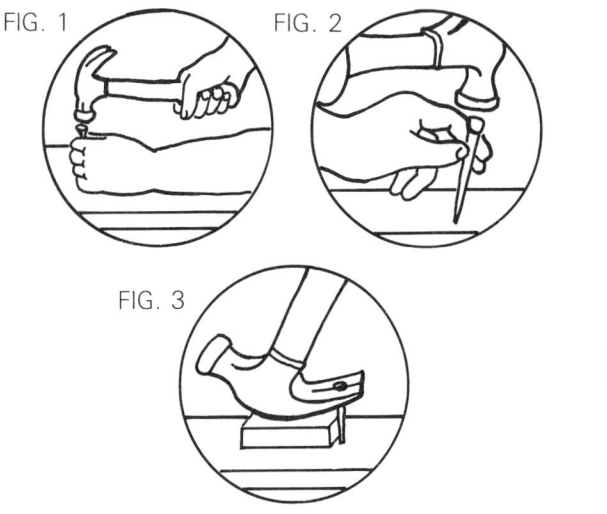

a What is the effect of holding a hammer near the end of the handle?
_____

b Why should you use a nail punch?
_____

c What is the purpose of the claw end of a hammer?
_____

7 Look carefully at these illustrations showing the uses of slip-joint pliers. Read the statements below. Write *T* if the statement is true, *F* if it is false.

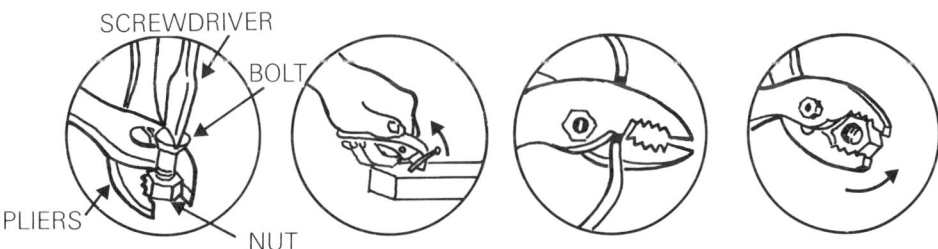

____ **a** While you turn a bolt with a screwdriver, slip-joint pliers can hold a nut.
____ **b** Pliers should not be used for straightening bent nails.
____ **c** Pliers can be used to bend or cut wire.
____ **d** Never use pliers for turning nuts.

8 Write step-by-step directions describing the illustrated flow chart below. Remember to write complete sentences.

First step: _____

_____

Second step: _____

_____

Last step: _____

_____

HOW TO LAY VINYL FLOOR TILES

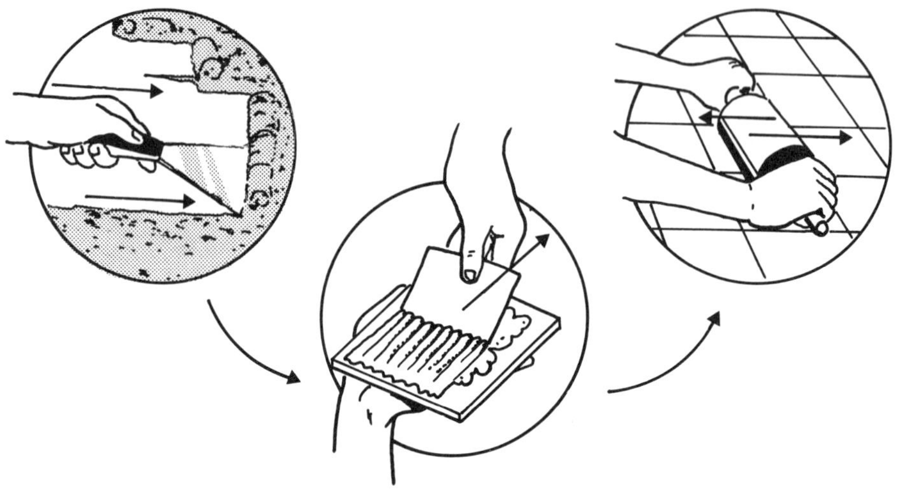

9 Which sentences are complete? Which ones are fragments or parts of sentences? Write *S* beside each complete sentence. Write *F* beside each fragment.

How to replace a broken window

____ **a** Work from the outside of the frame

____ **b** To remove broken glass with pliers and avoid cutting your fingers

____ **c** Old putty removed

____ **d** Place a thin ribbon of putty in the frame

____ **e** New glass firmly placed against the putty

10 Rewrite the directions in question 9 in paragraph form. Remember to make all fragments into complete sentences.

_____

_____

_____

_____

_____

_____

_____

_____

_____

_____

_____

_____

_____

Unit 6 Active/outdoor jobs

Many people do not like jobs in offices or factories. They prefer outside jobs which keep them active. Some of these jobs require special qualifications and training; others do not. If qualifications are required, you will find some information in this unit. Reading and writing skills are, of course, needed in all these jobs at some time.

Forecourt sales staff   80
Pricing and estimating petrol deliveries

Delivery person   82
Reading maps

Building worker   84
What qualifications?

Glazier   86
Measuring and pricing glass

General farm worker   88
Training, answering ads

Revision   90

Forecourt sales staff

Forecourt sales staff have *varied* jobs. If the petrol station is *automated*, you might operate the *console*. You might also be the cashier. There may also be a forecourt attendant. He/she would check tyres, change oil and keep the forecourt clean and tidy. The attendant also checks in new supplies of petrol. In non-automatic forecourts the attendant does the cashier's *and* attendant's jobs. In either case, you might be expected to do shift work. This section deals with the skills needed by forecourt staff.

*Read the **Words you need**. Study the information given. Then answer the questions.

Words you need

automated run automatically by machine

console display unit (which tells you the amount of petrol used and the price)

dip check the contents with a dipstick

discount money off; reduction

varied of different kinds; changing

PETROL	
2 STAR **	£2.00 per gallon
3 STAR ***	£2.03 per gallon
4 STAR ****	£2.05 per gallon
OIL	
1 LITRE	£1.30
DISCOUNT ON 4 GALLONS OF PETROL OR MORE – 20p	

? Questions

1 A customer buys 4 gallons of 3 star petrol. How much will this cost? How much change will she get from £10?
   a Cost _____
   b Change _____

2 A disabled driver asks you for help. You check his tyres, battery and radiator. Then you give him 3 gallons of 2 star. How much will this cost?

80

3 A customer buys 2 gallons of 4 star and 1 litre of oil. How much is the bill?

4 Your petrol station sells accessories and sweets too. A customer asks for a bar of chocolate (30p) and a set of sparking plugs (4 in a set at 90p each). How much does this cost?

5 Kay's hours are unusual. She works 8 a.m. to 3 p.m. one day. Next day she works 3 p.m. to 10 p.m. She has the third day off. She works weekends too. Out of 9 days how many days does she work? And how many hours?

_____ days
_____ hours

6 A customer wants to pay by credit card. She then asks for discount. This is only allowed on cash sales. What would you says to her? (Be polite!)

7 What do you think are the advantages and disadvantages of working at a petrol station? Write them down here:
Advantages _____

Disadvantages _____

8 The forecourt sales staff must check in new supplies. Then the statement of delivery must be signed as correct. One tanker holds 6000 gallons. The attendant checks and finds that 5190 gallons have gone in. How many gallons short is the delivery?

9 You operate a console at a self-service station. A customer takes out the nozzle before selecting the grade of petrol. Therefore it won't work. What advice would you give the customer over the speaker system? Write out your advice below:

10 Imagine you are the owner of a non-automated service station. You wish to take on a young person to serve and take cash. What qualities would you be looking for? Write them down here:

11 You are an attendant at a petrol station. A delivery of petrol arrives. You check the contents of the tanker with a dipstick. After unloading you check the tanker again. Why?

12 Would you wipe the dipstick before using it? Why?

Delivery person

Delivery people should be able to read maps. They should, of course, know road signs. Time can be saved on deliveries if the map is studied beforehand. There is skill in loading too. Imagine the last item to be delivered is heavy, you wouldn't want it at the back of the van. You would put it at the front of the van, that way you wouldn't be lifting it on and off all the time.

This section gives practice in the skills that delivery people need. In particular, it should help in learning to use an A–Z directory.

*Look at the **Words you need**. Make sure you know them. Study the map and instructions from the A–Z directory. Then answer the questions.

Words you need

access approach; way in
directory guide; book of directions
map reference number and letter of a place on a map

Ave. Avenue
Cres. Crescent
La. Lane
Rd. Road
St. Street

Use of A–Z index

A strict alphabetical order is followed, e.g. Mab Rd. comes before Mab St. but after Mab Ave. Each road is followed by its map reference, e.g. Bull Hotel 2A 48 means square 2A on page 48.

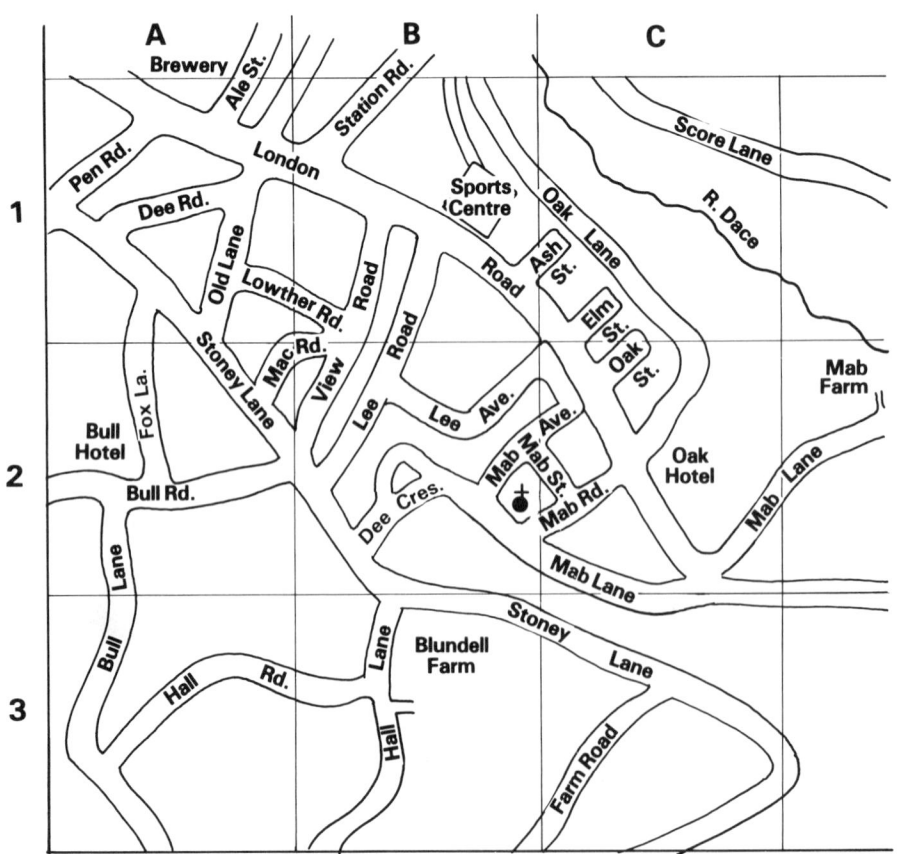

? Questions

1 Sort these four roads into alphabetical order. Add their map references.
   Hall Rd.,
   Lee Rd.,
   Hall La.,
   Lee Ave.

   1 _____
   2 _____
   3 _____
   4 _____

Study the map taken from the A–Z directory. Answer the questions.

2 In what square will you find the sports centre?
   _____

3 You are delivering beer from the brewery. First you must go to the Bull Hotel. Write down the route for the driver, starting with Ale Street.
   Ale St. left into _____
   _____
   _____
   _____

4 You see this sign at the corner of Ash Street. What does it mean?
   _____

5 There is no road between Score Lane and Oak Lane. Why do you think this is so?
   _____
   _____

6 In what square will you find Blundell Farm?
   _____

7 What does the sign above mean?
   a Access restricted
   b No entry
   c No overtaking
   d No goods vehicles.

8 You break down at the corner of Bull Lane and Hall Road. You phone the boss and ask him to send help. He asks in what square in the A–Z you can be found. What square should you say?
   _____

9 From the Bull Hotel you have to go to the Oak Hotel. Write down the route below:
   _____
   _____
   _____
   _____

10 One afternoon you have deliveries for Oak Street and Oak Lane. Can you go through Oak Street into Oak Lane?
   _____

11 The map shows a church in square B2. It is at the junction of two roads. Write down the names of the two roads.
   _____
   _____

12 You are delivering furniture to the following places:
   a 3 piece suite to Blundell Farm;
   a bed to Old Lane;
   a coffee table to the Sports Centre;
   a bedside cabinet to Mab Farm.
   Your first call is Old Lane. In which order will you deliver the goods? Name the goods.
   1st _____
   2nd _____
   3rd _____
   4th _____

83

Building worker

Building workers need to be practical people. They must be interested in working with their hands. Most building jobs require fitness and the ability to do hard work. The traditional ways of getting into the building industry were as follows: you could apply direct to a building firm; or you could apply to the Construction Industry Training Board (CITB). But now CITB offers training under the Youth Training Scheme (YTS). The skills needed vary from job to job. All jobs need a knowledge of tools and materials, and measuring skills. Often reading job lists and short instructions will be required. This section will give you some idea of the skills needed.

*Read the **Words you need**. Learn them if you don't know them. Study *Training for school-leavers* and *Work and qualifications in the building industry*. Then answer the questions.

Words you need

academic   relating to subjects studied at school and college
general operative   person who does the unskilled jobs
guaranteed   assured of; certain
qualifications   training and knowledge; certificates
technician   skilled scientific or industrial worker

Training for school-leavers

The CITB asks employers to help provide planned work experience for YTS trainees. This will be on site or in offices with periods of off-site training. Training is given at technical colleges or training centres. Trainees will be given an introduction to the industry. After that trainees will be selected for further training. Some will be trained for skills at technician, craft or general operative level. By the end of the year, some will be selected for employment as apprentices.

Work and qualifications in the building industry

Job	Type of work	Qualifications
General operative	General lifting and carrying to help craftsmen. Digging, helping with concreting.	Not academic. Need to be fit and strong. Ready to work hard in tough conditions. A head for heights.
Plant operator	Operating trucks, tractors, dumpers, etc.	Must be over 18. Need a driving licence.
Craftsman	Plastering; roofing; tiling; bricklaying; scaffolding; decorating; electrical work, etc.	Good all-round education. 3–4 years training needed.
Technician	Preparing/inspecting jobs. Planning and pricing.	'O' levels or CSE 1s. Maths, science and English.

? Questions

1. What qualifications are required for a general operative's job?

2. Name the traditional ways of getting into the building industry.

3. In the puzzle below are twelve building jobs. Can you find them? Draw a ring around each one. Now write them on the lines on the right.

```
B R I C K L A Y E R S
P H D A G A X A L S C
L R E R M B E L E C A
A O C P R O S T C R F
S O O E N U I E T E F
T F R N U R O W R B O
E E A T E E J V I M L
R R T E Z R X O C U D
E Y O R T V P N I L E
R F R R E T N I A P R
R E L I T J O I N E R
```

1 _____   7 _____
2 _____   8 _____
3 _____   9 _____
4 _____   10 _____
5 _____   11 _____
6 _____   12 _____

4. How long does training take for a craftsman?

5. What qualifications does a technician need to be accepted for training?

6. Name two jobs a general operative might do on a building site:

7. What jobs might a general operative move on to after the age of 18?

8. Look in Yellow Pages. See how many building firms there are in your area. Write some of them down below:
   Name   Address

9. What qualifications are needed for plant operators?

10. YTS trainees might train at Technical College or Training Centre. Where else might they receive training?

11. Think of the advantages and the disadvantages of these jobs. Write down one example of each:

Job	Advantage	Disadvantage
Plasterer		
Bricklayer		
Electrician		
Scaffolder		
Technician		
General operative		

Glazier

Some glaziers learn their trade through an apprenticeship others may learn through YTS. Most learn their skills from 'on-the-job' training. Glaziers have to be accurate at measuring and have to make careful notes of measurements. Later, these must be read accurately. Glaziers learn to work skilfully with glass. They must know the skills of *cutting* glass, *puttying*, and using *beading*. They will learn about different weights of glass and patterned glass. They must know how to work out prices. This section gives you some idea of a glazier's work.

*Read the **Words you need**. Read *Replacing a broken window*. Then answer the questions.

Words you need

beading thin strips of moulded wood to hold windows in place
expansion stretching; spreading out
pliable softened; easily shaped

putty a kind of paste cement
rebate the edge of a frame, may be cut back or grooved
sprigs small, headless nails

Replacing a broken window

Remove old putty with a hacking knife.
Make sure the rebate is clear of old putty and sprigs.
Measure the inside of the window frame.
Now cut the glass 3 mm short of these measurements.
Next work the putty until pliable by rolling it between the fingers. (Moisten it with a little linseed oil if it becomes hard.)
Paint the rebate with priming paint to stop the putty cracking.
Press small pieces of putty round the rebate frame.
Place the glass in position, pressing it into the putty.
Level off the putty with a knife. (Allow to set before cleaning.)

Note: Never fit new glass too tight against the frame. You must allow for expansion of the timber.
Instead of puttying, beading can be used. This may not be as waterproof as putty. Beading is better used for inside jobs.

  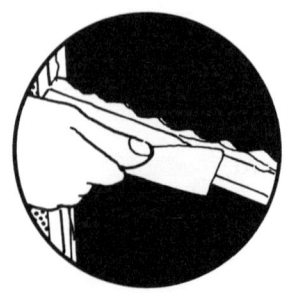 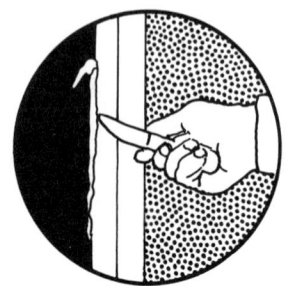

? Questions

1. What do you need to make putty softer?

2. How is putty made pliable?

3. A window frame measures 1m × 70cm. What measurements should the glass be cut to?

4. Before glazing, the rebate is painted with priming paint. Why?

5. Look below at the instructions for replacing a broken window. You will notice the sequence is out of order. Write out the sentences in the correct order:

   Cut the glass 3mm short of the measure.
   Measure the window frame all round.
   Place the glass in position.
   Work the putty between the fingers to make it pliable.

   i _____
   ii _____
   iii _____
   iv _____

6. Glass costs £6.30 per square metre. How much will a pane 3m × 2m cost?

7. Why is the glass not cut to the same size as the frame?

8. Glass is sometimes cut across corners as in the drawing below:

   Why do you think glass is cut this way?

9. You are a glazier's assistant. You are in the shop and receive the following telephone call:

   This is T. Jones of 394 Old St. Last night our rear bedroom windows were blown in by the gale. Could you send someone to repair them today? One window measures 1.5m × 1m. The other one is 1.5m × 75cm. I shall leave the keys next door at number 392.

   Write out the necessary information and instructions on the pad opposite.

EEZY GLAZE   410 New Rd.
Memo Pad

From:

Address:

Order:

Other information:

General farm worker

Farmers today need lots of skills. More and more machines are being used on farms. New *techniques* and increased knowledge call for more training. Much has to be learned, for instance, about new *fertilizers*. Good general farm workers must be *adaptable*. They may be hauling and stacking bales, lifting bulbs, hop-picking, etc. They may need to drive and operate machines. Often people get interested in farm work through *casual* holiday work. This section will help you think about the skills needed.

*Read the **Words you need**. Study the chart, the ads and the information given. Then answer the questions.

Words you need

agricultural relating to farming
adaptable versatile; able to tackle many jobs
arable fit for growing crops
casual occasional; seasonal
fertilizers chemicals to enrich the soil
module unit; task
specific precise; relating to one thing
supervisor overseer; chargehand
techniques skills; ways of working

Information on training

A general farm worker's training used to be unplanned. But now the Agricultural Training Board offers regular training. Their regional officers help employers train workers through a system of modules. That is, they develop one specific skill at a time. For instance, milking. When you pass that test you start another module. That way you can build up the skills you need. More than one module can be taken at one time. When you are ready, you can take a supervisor's course.

Farming Chart

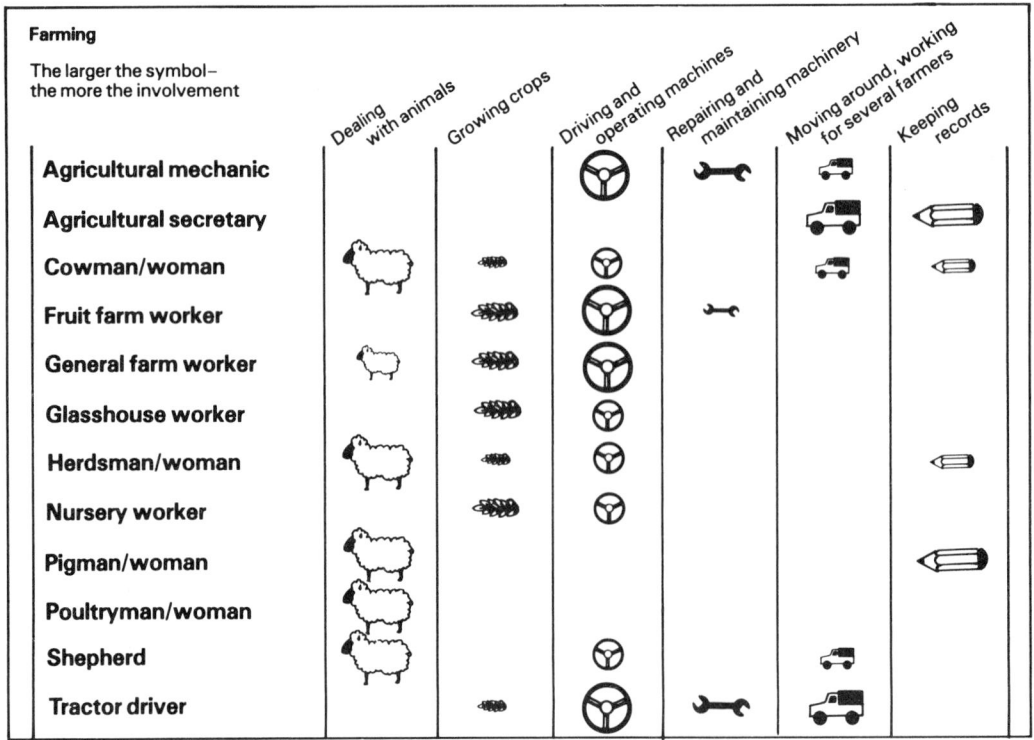

? Questions

Looking at the farming chart, answer the questions.

1 After some years as a general farm worker you may want to specialize. If you become an agricultural mechanic, what jobs would you do?

_____
_____
_____

2 Which specialized farm jobs require the keeping of records?

_____
_____
_____
_____

A
General Farm Worker
Required for 226 acre arable and pig farm. The crops are potatoes, sugar beet and corn. Could be some tractor work. Assist with pig feeding. Accommodation available. Phone (974) 9898.

B
General Farm Worker
1200 acre farm (arable). To work with beef and all modern machinery. Training will be given for caterpillar driving if necessary. Write with details and references: P. Duff & Sons, Crosby Farm, Hightown.

---

3 Look at ads A and B above. Which animals do these farms rear?
Farm A _____
Farm B _____

4 Which crops are grown on farm A?
_____

5 Which ad suggests that training will be given?
_____

6 Can you name a piece of machinery a tractor might pull on an arable farm?
_____

7 Name some of the jobs a general farm worker might do.
_____
_____
_____
_____

8 You may not often use reading skills as a farmer. However, at times they will be most important. What might happen, for instance, if you misread instructions on a fertilizer pack?
_____
_____

9 If you were training for job A above, what modules would you need?
_____
_____
_____

10 Job A offers accommodation. Do you think this might be important in attracting farm workers? Why?
_____
_____

11 You have not had a permanent farm job before. What experience might help you get one of these jobs?
_____
_____
_____

12 Which of the two jobs above do you think you would prefer? Can you say why?
_____
_____

89

Revision

1 Do you know the meanings of these words? Write them on the lines after the word.

discount _____

access _____

restricted _____

guaranteed _____

pliable _____

casual _____

specific _____

2 These road names should be in alphabetical order. Number them in their correct order.

Scots Street _____

Scots Road _____

Scotsman Lane _____

Scotsman Avenue _____

3 Match the workers you have read about in this unit with the sentences below. Write their jobs on the lines provided.

a Work the putty until pliable.

_____

b Take the tractor into the field.

_____

c Look up the directions in your A–Z.

_____

d I want you to help with the concreting.

_____

e How much is the 2-star?

_____

4 These abbreviations are found in this unit. What do they mean? Write them in full on the lines provided.

St. _____

CITB _____

_____

ad. _____

Rd. _____

Ave. _____

La. _____

mm. _____

m. _____

5a Here is a plan of a window frame. Write down here the size of glass a glazier would cut to fit this:

_____

2.25 m

2 m

b Why would the glass be cut smaller than the frame?

_____

6 Name the qualifications required for a technician in the building trade:

_____

_____

_____

_____

7 Below is a list of jobs done by some building craftsmen. But they are jumbled up! Can you unravel them? Write them out correctly on the lines provided.

scoldaffer _____

ickbrayler _____

lastperer _____

recodator _____

liter _____

foorer _____

tricianecel _____

noijer _____

lumpber _____

azglier _____

8 Look at the A–Z map on page 82. Someone wants to get from Mab Farm to the Bull Hotel. Write out your directions on the lines below:

_____
_____
_____
_____
_____

9 General farm workers are usually employed in three main tasks. Can you name them?

_____
_____
_____

10 You are going to replace a friend's broken window. Write out a list of the things you will need:

_____   _____
_____   _____
_____   _____
_____   _____

11 Below is an extract from the index of an A–Z directory.

Mab Ave.	2B 48
Mab La.	2B 2C 48
Mab Rd.	2B 2C 48
Mab St.	2B 48
Mabel Rd.	1A 1B 50
Mabel St.	1B 50
Macauley St.	2A 19
Macarthur Rd.	3C 25
Mace Ave.	1C 2

On which page and square will you find the following?
Mab St. _____
Macauley St. _____
Mab Rd. _____
Mabel Rd. _____

12 Remember the work on abilities and characteristics in Unit 1? Think of the abilities and characteristics needed in the following jobs. By each one write out what you think they require.

Job	Abilities	Characteristics
Forecourt sales staff		
Delivery person		
Building labourer		
Glazier		
General farm worker		

13 Imagine that you are a bricklayer. The boss has gone away and left some written instructions. Unfortunately, the rain has spoiled the message. See if you can understand the message. Write it out below.

John,
 First take 200 br
up to the brickla
who are building th
outer wall.
 When you've fin
start the ceme   xer
Then you can he Joe
and Tom with the
con   g.
        Mr. J

Message
John,
_____
_____
_____
_____
_____
_____
_____
_____
_____
_____

14 Imagine that you have done some general farm work in the holidays. You also have a driving licence. Write out a letter of application for job A on page 89. Look back to Unit 2 and check that you know the correct layout. Write out your letter in the space below.

Unit 7 Artistic jobs

Some people are good at creating things. Such people may have a lot of artistic ability. They may have a good eye for pattern and design. Artistic jobs also require reading and writing skills. Some of these jobs require training, either 'on the job' or through an apprenticeship or a full-time course at college. The skills in this unit will be helpful if you take up one of these jobs. Even if you don't, they could help you develop some home hobbies.

Hairdresser   **94**
Outlining directions in sequence

Florist's assistant   **96**
Receiving and writing instructions

Photographer   **98**
Following film and camera instructions

Dressmaker   **100**
Using a pattern

Signwriter   **102**
Using writing skills

Revision   **104**

Hairdresser

Hairdressers learn their trade through an apprenticeship, full-time college course or YTS.

Outlining directions in sequence

Directions for using hair products are often too complicated to remember easily. Think of hairdressers giving a perm for the first time for example. They must recognize all the steps in a process and *outline* them in *sequence*. Outlining helps you in jobs where complex directions must be followed. This section helps you to follow complex directions.

*Read the **Words you need**. Make sure you understand them. Read the tips for outlining complex directions. Then answer the questions.

Words you need

complicated complex; difficult; involved
lather form a foam
neutraliser liquid used to stop a chemical reaction
outline show the main features or stages in directions
sequence the order in which things happen

Tips for outlining complex directions

- Write a title. It should state the purpose of the directions.
- Identify the main steps and number them in sequence. Use Roman numerals (I, II, III, IV, etc.).
- Identify the in-between or smaller steps under the main steps. List them in sequence. Use capital letters for these steps.

? Questions

1 Read the directions in paragraph form below. Then study the outline on the right that was made by a hairdresser. Write the last two small steps on the lines provided.

HONEY PLUS is a two-step process of shampooing and conditioning the hair. First shampoo by applying the yellow liquid onto wet hair. Lather and then rinse with warm water. Next, condition the hair by working the green liquid into it. Rinse after waiting for five minutes. Towel-dry the hair.

Outline:

Using HONEY PLUS } *title*

I Shampoo } *main step*

   A Wet hair
   B Apply yellow liquid } *in-between steps*
   C Lather
   D Rinse

II Condition

   A Work green liquid through
   B Wait five minutes
   C _____
   D _____

Looks-Natural Perm

● Excellent for every type of hair, except extra-dry or tinted. Be sure to examine the hair first. If it is extra-dry or tinted, use LOOKS-NATURAL PERM – SPECIAL.

● Make sure which perm lotion to use. Wash the hair using a mild shampoo. Make sure that you rinse the hair thoroughly. Then dry the hair with a towel.

● The size of the rods you use is important. On it depends the amount of body and curl. Select the right rods.

● *The curling or processing.*
Begin by parting the hair into three sections: the neckline and lower back; the front area from ear to ear; and the crown area. When this is done, apply the lotion about 3 cm from the scalp. Start with the area on the neckline. Apply lotion to one curl at a time and wind the hair. Wind all the hair in this section. Do the same with the other two sections.

● Immediately unwind the test curl. For normal and fine hair, the next tests are done every three minutes. For bleached, tinted or extra-dry hair, test every minute until you get the desired wave or curl.

● Finally, rinse the curls thoroughly for three minutes. Use comfortably hot water. Without removing the rods, blot each curl with a towel. Apply the neutraliser to each curl, working from top to bottom. Repeat the application to top of curls. Wait for five minutes before removing the rods. Apply the remaining neutraliser to curls. Gently massage the hair with the palms of hands. Rinse the hair with warm water and towel dry.

2 As a hairdresser you certainly want to satisfy the customer. You need to understand the directions for using a hair product. Read the directions above for giving a 'Looks-Natural' perm. Then complete the outline below. Be sure to write the steps in the correct sequence.

Giving a permanent wave
   I The three steps before starting the perm:
      A _____
      B _____
      C _____
   II The steps to follow in curling the hair:
      A _____
      B _____
      C _____
   III Testing:
   IV The last steps after waving:
      _____
      _____

3 Which perm is said to be needed for extra-dry hair?
_____

4 A customer wants to know how long it takes to do a perm. How long, roughly, does the Looks-Natural Perm take? (Work it out from the instructions.)
_____

Florist's assistant

There are some college courses for florists, but most train 'on the job'. They have to learn about different flowers and plants. They have to arrange flowers for displays in hotels, offices, churches, etc. They need to master the skills of making *wreaths* and *bouquets*. Orders have to be taken, sometimes over the phone. These must be written down and repeated for accuracy. Handwriting must be neat. Florists have to write messages on cards to accompany the flowers. This section is about some of the reading and writing skills that florists need.

*Read the **Words you need**. Study the information given and answer the questions.

Words you need

bouquet   bunch of flowers
recipient   one who receives
requirements   what is needed

sheaf   bundle (of flowers)
wreath   circle of flowers and leaves entwined together

Taking orders over the phone

Many orders are given over the phone. A customer may ask for flowers (a wreath, sheaf or bouquet) to be made up. The florist needs to know how much the customer wants to pay. The customer may ask for particular flowers to be used. The florist will need to note the following:

a   the caller's name and address;
b   type of flowers required and the cost;
c   name and address of recipient;
d   date and time flowers are required;
e   the message that is to be written and sent with the flowers.

? Questions

Below is a florist's order pad. Look at the information given. Now answer the questions.

Order Pad
From: Jim Prescot
Address: 2 Oak Road
Name of recipient: Esther Swede
Requirements: 1 doz. red roses (£6)
Send to: 4 Blundell Lane
Date & time required: 8am. 28th Jan
Message: Happy Birthday Esther, Love Jim

1   What is the name and address of the caller?

2a   What is the name and address of the recipient?

b   When are the flowers required?

3 Florists' handwriting has to be neat. Can you write out the message from the pad on page 96? Write it on the card below. Use your best writing.

4 Some people need help from the florist when choosing their flowers. Look at the list of prices below. A lady wants a sheaf for about £3.50. Make one up. Write down your selection, prices and bill below:

_____ _____
_____ _____
_____ _____
_____ _____
_____TOTAL _____

Price List	
Red Roses	50p each
Carnations	35p each
Chrysanthemums	30p each
Tulips	25p each
Gipsy Grass	15p
Ferns	15p

5 Look at the price list above. A man wants a bouquet sent to his girl friend. He asks for four of each flower and some gipsy grass and ferns. How much will this cost?

6 If a florist does not repeat the order, things can go wrong. Compare the order pad below with the original on the previous page. Write down here what is wrong:

_____
_____
_____

Order Pad
From: Jim Prescot
Address: 2 Old Road
Name of recipient: Esther Swede
Requirements: 1 dog, red roses (£6)
Send to: 14 Blundell Lane
Date & time required: 8a.m. 29th Jan
Message: Happy Birthday Jim
Love Esther

7 A man asks for a wreath to be made up. It is for an old aunt who has just died. He asks if you would write a suitable message on the card. Her name is Anne. Write it below:

Photographer

Some photographers are self-taught, but many do training courses which are available at various colleges. The work of photographers is very skilful. Besides knowing how to *focus* a camera, they must learn other skills. They should know how to set the *adjustments* for various lights and distances. Photographers will learn about *filters* and *light meters*. They may also develop their own photographs and use an *enlarger*. This section will help you learn about photography. Even if you don't become a photographer, the knowledge is useful.

*Read and learn the **Words you need**. Study the information on photography. Then see if you can answer the questions.

Words you need

adjustments alterations
ASA scale and **degrees DIN** speed of the film
developer chemical which brings out the picture
enlarger instrument which makes prints larger
filter disc of glass which modifies colours
focus get a sharp image

lens aperture opening through which light passes
lens hood cover, shading the lens from direct sunlight
light meter instrument for measuring brightness of light
negative film which carries the reverse of the print
shutter speed speed at which the lens aperture is opened and closed

Information on camera adjustment

Some cameras have many adjustments. However, the principles of photography are the same for all cameras. Three adjustments must be made: 1) to the *focus* so that the picture will not be blurred; 2) to the *lens aperture* and 3) *shutter speed* to give correct exposure. The following are extras that may give you more refined pictures. A *close-up lens* allows you to focus on very near objects. *Filters* make some colours lighter or darker. When dark, *flash guns* can be used, and their own built-in *light meters* which set the shutter and lens automatically.

Information on how to obtain good pictures

1 Always hold the camera level.
2 Find the object in the viewfinder.
3 Slowly squeeze the shutter button without shaking.
4 Do not photograph near objects without a close-up lens.
5 Do not always put your main object in the centre of the picture.
6 Choose plain backgrounds. Avoid lines in the background (such as poles, fences, etc.).
7 Try to contrast the main object with the background (i.e. black background for a white main object).

? Questions

1. What three adjustments have to be made when using a camera?

2. What do the markings 'ASA' or 'DIN' on a pack of film mean?

3. You are taking a photograph in very bright sunshine. Would you use:
   a a flash;
   b a filter;
   c a long exposure;
   d a large aperture?

4. To develop films you must follow the correct order of doing things. The following list is out of order. Can you show the correct order by putting a number by each phrase?
   ___ Negative is put in the enlarger.
   ___ The print is developed.
   ___ Light falls on the film.
   ___ The print is fixed, washed and dried.
   ___ Film is put in the developer.
   ___ Prints are made from the negative.

5. You want to photograph a racing car moving at high speed. Would you need a long or a short exposure time?

6. You are taking a picture of your friend who is wearing a white shirt. Which of these backgrounds would you choose, and why?
   a white background
   b black background

7. What do you use to find out which exposure you need?

8. You want to take a close-up. What do you need to use?

9. Some cameras give settings for groups/views and close-ups. What setting should you use for groups of people: more than 2.5 metres, or less?

10. You may have to read film instructions. Sometimes symbols are used instead of words. Draw the following symbols by the correct instruction:

    Hazy sunshine

    Bright sunshine

    Cloudy/dull

    Cloudy/clear intervals

11. You take a photograph and shake the camera. What do you think might happen to the film? How will it turn out?

12. The information on taking photographs tells you to avoid lines in the background. Why do you think this is good advice?

Dressmaker

Dressmakers usually learn their trade 'on the job'.

Using a pattern

The clothing industry includes a wide variety of jobs. They vary from retail selling to clothing manufacture, dressmaking and tailoring. A basic understanding of how a garment is put together is *vital*. Dressmakers and tailors need this knowledge. This section is about some of the skills needed by dressmakers.

*Read the **Words you need**. Read the instructions and study the diagram. See if you can answer the questions.

Words you need

baste sew with long, loose stitches
garment article of clothing
grain direction of the threads in a piece of fabric

View A, B, C the variations in style that can be made with one pattern
vital very important, essential

A pattern is another type of diagram. A clothing pattern is a diagram that has been divided into several pieces. All the pieces fit together to form the garment.

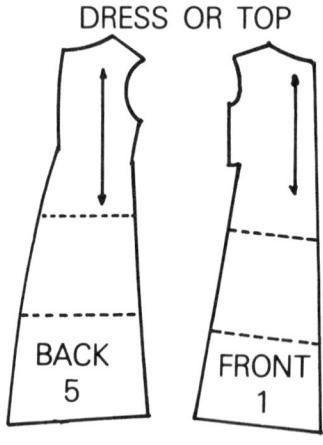

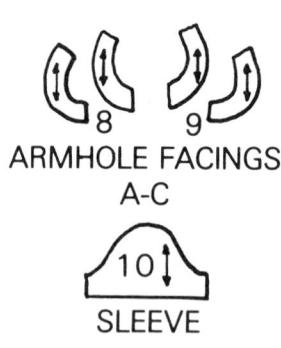

The key to the symbols
The instructions that come with the pattern have a key. This explains the symbols used on the pattern pieces.

Grain line This line is placed on the fabric in the same direction as the grain.

Notches Before basting, pieces are pinned together so that the notches line up.

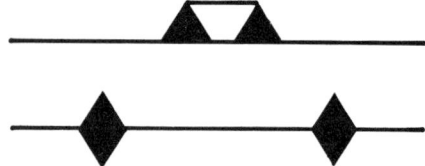

Fold To cut two of something, the fabric is folded in half before laying out the pattern. The arrows are placed on the folded edge of the fabric.

Cutting line The piece is cut along this line.

Transfer markings Make these markings on the fabric using tailor's chalk, thread or a tracing wheel.

Seam line This is the stitching line – usually 15 mm from the edge of the pattern piece.

? Questions

1. What do we mark cloth with (for the pockets, to match seams, etc.)?

2. How far is the seam line stitched from the edge of the pattern?

3. Read each statement below. If the statement is true, write *T* on the blank. If the statement is false, write *F*. Use the pattern piece on this page to help you give the correct answer.
   a ____ The pattern piece illustrated is to be placed on the folded edge of the fabric.
   b ____ After cutting, the two front pieces will have to be sewn together.
   c ____ The piece is cut along the broken line.
   d ____ The dart is stitched outwards to the cut edge of the fabric.
   e ____ The dress shown in View C is longer than the one shown in View B.
   f ____ The pattern shown is for a larger woman.
   g ____ The shoulder is stitched from the neck edge to the armhole edge.
   h ____ For View C, the side seam is stitched to the circle.
   i ____ When stitching seams, follow the direction of the arrows.
   j ____ When stitching darts, follow the solid line.

4. Have you got the qualities needed to be a dressmaker? What are they?

Signwriter

Signwriters may serve an apprenticeship or learn through YTS. Some, however, may come into signwriting from other trades. Signwriting is a craft usually done by specialist firms. But often firms of painters and decorators employ a signwriter. Sometimes experienced signwriters set up their own business. Signwriters need a sense of design and drawing skills. *Legibility* of lettering is important in all writing. It is especially so for the job of signwriter. This section tells you about some of the skills of signwriting.

*Read the **Words you need**. Study the information on signwriting that is given. See if you can answer the questions.

Words you need

consistency thickness; density
cursive flowing; linked
formal writing unlinked script
legibility clearness; ease of reading

sans serif without serifs, e.g. n
serif short lines at the end of some letters, e.g. n

Information on signwriting

A signwriter has to learn about different paints. A knowledge of which paint to use on wood, iron and plastics is necessary. Sometimes paints will have to be mixed. This will be done in order to get the right colour and consistency. A knowledge of brushes and which to use for various jobs is needed too. Often the signwriter will work with letters made of different materials. Sometimes illuminated letters will be used. Sometimes a design will have to be painted as well as lettered.

An apprentice may start by painting the background of signs. This must be done carefully and smoothly. Without a smooth finish the letters will not stand out. An apprentice will work with an experienced signwriter who may draw letters for him to fill in. When skilful enough, the apprentice may be allowed to draw the letters. At first, simple block letters will be drawn. Later, more fancy lettering will be tackled. Finally, those with the skill may go on to draw designs. Signwriters may have to work in all sorts of places. Think of where you see signs, on the sides of boats, vans and buildings (even on the tops of buildings!), in hospitals and at the roadsides.

? Questions

1 Draw serifs on these letters below:

a b d l n
f h k m q

2 Why are paints sometimes mixed?

3 Name two places where you might see signwriters at work.

4 The opposite of legibility is 'illegibility'. What does it mean?

5 Which do you think is easier to read, cursive or formal writing?

_____

6 You are writing a name on a window. It is on the inside and must be written in reverse. This name is in reverse. Write it out as you would normally see it.

John Lewis

_____

7 You want to be a signwriter. Which subjects may be helpful to you at school?

_____

8 You are an apprentice signwriter. You gradually learn the following skills, beginning with the easiest. They are not in order. Put them in order as you would learn them. Place a number 1–4 by each one.

____ Drawing designs
____ Writing block letters
____ Filling in block letters
____ Fancy lettering

9 Roman lettering has thick down strokes and thin up strokes. Draw these letters in Roman letters (capitals):

m   v   w   k   n

10 Look at these names. Which one is better spaced? Say why.

a W I L L I A M   **b** WILLIAM

_____

11 You are a signwriter. You have to paint a sign on a shop front. The boss asks you to paint the letters in gold leaf. Why must you take extra care with this job?

_____

12 A signwriter needs many qualities. How many can you think of? Write them here:

_____
_____
_____
_____

13 Imagine you are a signwriter. You have been asked to design for British Rail. They want you to use the slogan 'This is the age of the train'. On your poster below take great care with the lettering. Make sure it is attractive and well balanced.

Revision

1 Synonyms
Underline one word which means the same as the first word. The first one is done for you.
complex same, <u>complicated</u>, sequence.
cursive capitals, small, flowing.
legibility clearness, thickness, darkness.
vital lost, expensive, essential.
adjustments settings, clothes, collections.
required needed, suggested, hoped.

2 The following instructions are out of order. Write them in order on the lines below:
To obtain a good picture
Do not put your main object in the centre of the picture.
Slowly squeeze the shutter button.
Find the object in the viewfinder.
Hold the camera level.

  i _____
  ii _____
  iii _____
  iv _____

3 Give *one* word for the following phrases:
a one who receives _____
b the order in which things happen _____
c to get a sharp image _____
d sew with long, loose stitches _____
e short line at the end of a letter _____

4 You might send flowers on special occasions. The words below are special occasions, but they are jumbled. Can you write them out correctly on the lines provided?
laVentine's Day _____
Brithdya _____
istChrmas _____
oMther's Dya _____
aFer'sth Day _____
eddWing _____
pratsie _____
annerivsary _____

5 Two words in each sentence below are out of place. Write these two words on the line at the end of the sentence:
a The come that instructions with the pattern have a key.
_____
b The line is placed on the direction in the same fabric as the grain.
_____
c The cut is piece along this line.
_____
d Before basting, pinned are pieces together.
_____

6 Place these steps for tinting hair in the correct sequence. Write the numbers 1 to 5 in the blanks provided.

___ Apply the tint first around the hairline and on the roots.
___ Then rinse the hair thoroughly until the water is clear.
___ Leave tint on the hair for a further 12 minutes.
___ After 15 minutes comb tint through to cover the hair.
___ To prepare for tints, shampoo the hair, then rinse and towel dry.

7 The following words are all spelled incorrectly. Can you write them out correctly? Write each one on the line after the word.

a Floorist _____
b Fotografer _____
c Herdresser _____
d Sine-writer _____
e Dressmacker _____
f kamera _____
g dyerections _____
h seekwence _____
i eksposure _____
j diergram _____
k owtline _____
l informashon _____

8 You send a message with some flowers for your friend's 18th birthday. Write out the message on the card on the right. Don't forget to sign it!

9 Rewrite these directions in outline form:

The condition of your hair can be improved by using Silky Locks Conditioner. To get the best results, follow the directions carefully. First, shampoo hair as usual. Apply shampoo generously and then rinse well. Lightly towel-dry. Next, apply conditioner. Work one capful into hair thoroughly. Leave for two minutes and rinse with lukewarm water.

Title: _____
I _____
  A _____
  B _____
  C _____
II _____
  A _____
  B _____
  C _____

10 A signwriter has written on the inside of a shop window. Here is the sign seen from inside the shop. Write it out as it looks from outside the shop.

| Kelsalls |
| for |
| Beds-Prams |

(shown mirrored in the image)

11 Photographers must understand symbols on cameras and film. By each of the symbols on the right write out their meaning. Choose from the list: close-up; cloudy; view; hazy sunshine; bright sunshine; group.

a ☀
b ⛰
c ☁
d 👥
e 🌅
f 👤

12 You work as a florist. A customer writes the following letter to you. Fill in the order form on the right with this information.

> 174 New Lane
> Oxford
> 3/4/84
>
> Dear Sir/Madam,
>
> Would you please send a bouquet (cost about £5.00) to Mr Jack Maddox, 14 Beach Lawn on 10th April before noon.
>
> Please include this message: 'Happy Sixtieth Birthday, Jack. Love from Joan and Victor.' Cheque enclosed.
>
> Yours faithfully
>
> V. Nethercott

Order Pad

From:

Address:

Name of recipient:

Requirements:

Send to:

Date & time required:

Message:

13 You are applying for a job as a signwriter with a local firm. You wish to impress by your handwriting. Write out your address, the date, greeting and first sentence in the space opposite.

Unit 8 Public service jobs

There are many different kinds of jobs in the public services. There are almost as many as there are in private business. Government jobs have good career opportunities for young people. The Community Volunteer Service, whilst not paying particularly well, does provide useful experience. All of these will demand some reading and writing skills.

Postman/postwoman   **108**
Aptitude tests and accuracy in checking

Police officer   **110**
Writing a factual report

Fireman/firewoman   **112**
Knowing the jargon and fire prevention

Armed services   **114**
Reading for essential meanings

Community Service Volunteers   **116**
Reading for main idea and details

Revision   **118**

Postman/postwoman

Postmen/postwomen have to collect, sort and deliver mail. They might work in a sorting office or on special inter-city sorting trains. Postmen/women might work on collection or deliveries. They might collect mail from post boxes. They might deliver mail on foot, by bike or van. A certain amount of reading is essential. Some writing skills are necessary too. The Post Office runs its own tests for these skills. This section gives you practice in some of these skills.

*Read the **Words you need** carefully. Read the information on being a postman/woman. Then answer the questions and try the aptitude test.

Words you need

aptitude   natural ability or skill
candidate   person applying for a job
deducted   taken away
mechanised   worked by machine

registered post   mail of which a written record is kept; if mail is lost, compensation can be claimed

Being a postman/woman

A postman/woman may start at the age of $16\frac{1}{2}$–18. At this age you are called a postal cadet. Cadets' duties are to take messages round the offices. After some months they learn about mail delivery. At 18 they become postmen/women. They must learn to deliver mail to houses and businesses. Later they may sort letters and packages. The work may also involve loading and unloading at railway stations. Postmen/women need to be fit and healthy. They often start early in the morning, and shift work is common.

The Post Office has a Youth Training Scheme. This offers training and work experience. It includes basic work skills and a minimum of 13 weeks off-the-job training. This is open to all 16-year-olds, and some unemployed 17-year-old school leavers.

Sorting may be done on special trains. Some offices are mechanised and postmen/women work on an automatic sorter. They feed letters into a machine which sorts them according to postcodes. The workers then bag and label the mail. Other postmen/women work in offices where sorting is done by hand. The mail is first sorted into large cities and counties. Then it is sorted again into districts. Finally it is sorted into individual streets and houses.

? Questions

1 What are the duties of a postal cadet?

2 Why do postmen/women need to be fit?

3 What are the duties of a postman/woman?

4 What is the difference between registered and ordinary mail?

5 Some addresses may be difficult to read. Look at the name and address on these envelopes. They have been defaced. See if you can fill in the full names and addresses:

| Mr Jo n Sm   h |
| 417 Chestnut R   d |
| B   ingham |

| Mis   A   ce Jo   s |
| 360 Man   ester S   t |
| L   don |
| Eng   nd |

Postman/woman aptitude test. There are usually three short written tests. Below are examples of two tests.

6 Same or Opposite Test
Look at the lines of words below. The first line is labelled 'SAME'. Two words in this line mean the same as each other. Find the two words and write their letter in the answer column. The second line is labelled 'OPPOSITE'. Find the two words which are opposites. Write down their letters in the answer column. Do each line in the same way.

			Answer
1	SAME	A surprised B complex C complicated D still E swift	B C
2	OPPOSITE	A loading B defaced C sorting D deduction E unloading	___ ___
3	SAME	A parcels B packages C mail D telegram E mistake	___ ___
4	SAME	A test B aptitude C candidate D ability E duties	___ ___
5	OPPOSITE	A punctual B ready C evening D never E late	___ ___
6	SAME	A daily B work C labourer D casual E occasional	___ ___

7 Test of Accuracy in Checking
Look at the names and addresses in column A. Now check the names and addresses which have been copied into column B. Where you find a mistake, draw a ring round it.

A	B
Mrs J P Spooner 17 Woodford Crescent NW 1	Mrs J P Spooner 17 Wodford Crescent NW 1
Mr G V Wright 51 Kimberley Drive, Oxford	Mr G V Wright 51 Kimberley Drive, Oxford
Mr R G S Gallacher 15 Greenside, Birmingham	Mr R G S Gallacker 5 Greenside, Birmingham
Miss D Torrington 133 Beckley Place, Hove	Mrs D Torrington 133 Beckley Place, Home

Police officer

All entrants to the police must sit an examination. Those successful will spend two years as probationer uniformed constables. Training at a police training school varies from 10–15 weeks. There may be further training and examinations at the end of probation. Police are recruited from people with good physique above the age of $18\frac{1}{2}$. In some parts of the country there are cadet schemes starting at $16\frac{1}{2}$.

Writing a factual report

Police officers have many duties. One is to get the facts about *illegal incidents*. Then a factual report must be written. The police officer must ask the right questions to get the facts. Written reports are very important. The information they contain helps the police make decisions. The police must decide if a crime has taken place. If so, then they must decide what action to take. Good writing skills are essential in this job. This section will help you to write factual reports.

*Read the **Words you need**. If you don't know them, read them several times. Read the reported incident below. Then read the tips for getting the facts. See if you can answer the questions.

Words you need

complainant person who reports a possibly illegal act
illegal against the law
incident event or happening
investigate make a study of

offence illegal act
suspect person who may have committed the illegal act
witness person who saw or heard the incident

Try this case

Suppose that you are on duty at the police station. It is the evening of 4 May. You receive the following phone call.

'Police? My name is George Larson. I live at 73 Park Drive. My house has been broken into. The TV, a diamond ring and £100 are gone. My wife and I just came back from shopping and found everything in a mess.'

You go round to the house and while you are there a neighbour, Helen Rice, calls. She says that she saw a man in a dark shirt and dark trousers getting into a light-coloured car. He seemed to be carrying something.

When you go to the house, this is what you see:

110

Tips for getting the facts

When police officers are investigating an incident, they could ask the five *W*s and one *H*.

Who was involved?   When did it happen?   Why did it happen?

What happened?   Where did it happen?   How did it happen?

? Questions

1 What questions do you think the police might ask Helen Rice?

_____
_____
_____
_____

2 The police will ask questions. What other investigations do you think they will make?

_____
_____
_____

3 Use the five *W*s and one *H* to write a report on the incident. Use all of the information given and include what you saw at the house. Write on the form below.

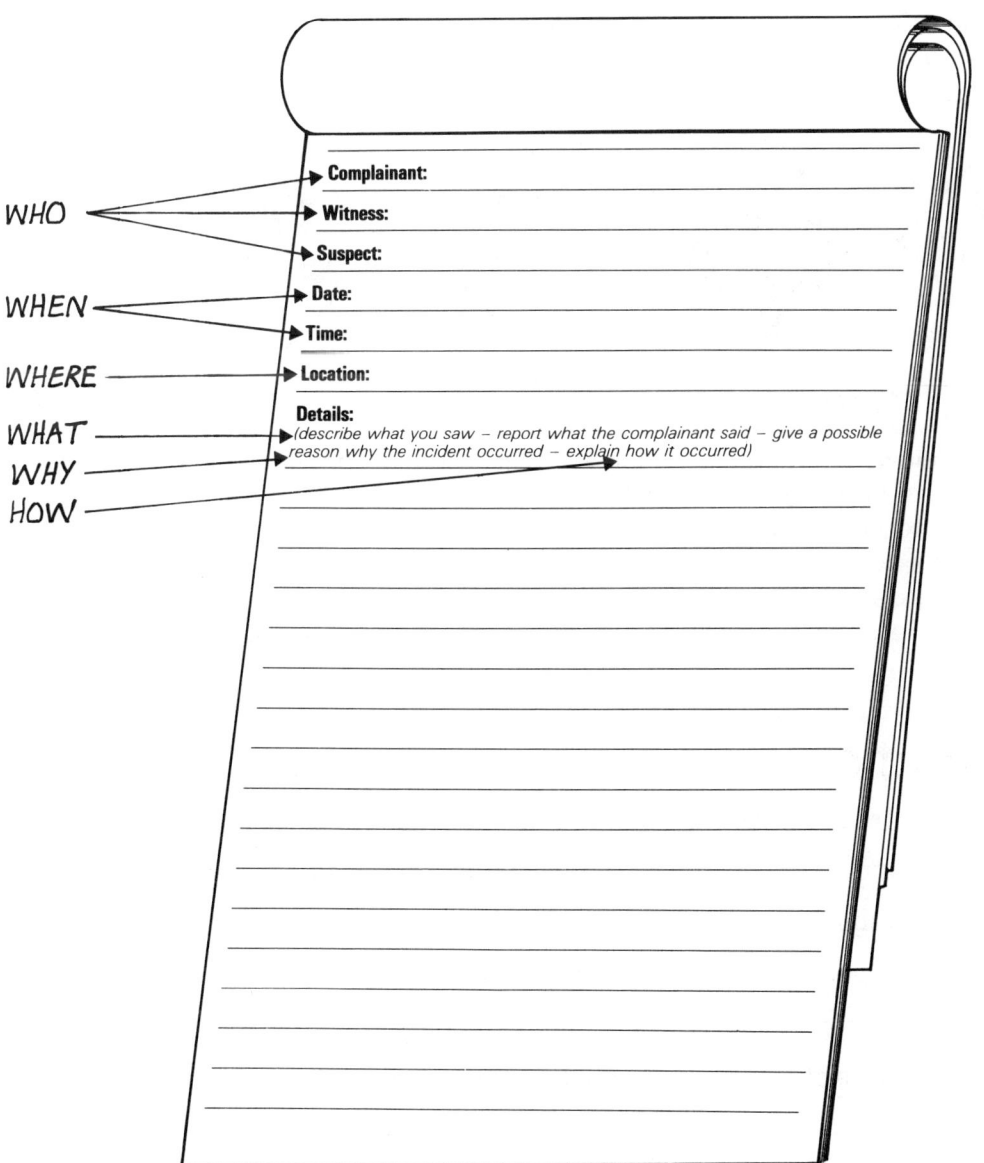

WHO → Complainant:
       → Witness:
       → Suspect:
WHEN → Date:
       → Time:
WHERE → Location:
WHAT ┐
WHY ├→ Details:
HOW ┘ (describe what you saw – report what the complainant said – give a possible reason why the incident occurred – explain how it occurred)

Fireman/firewoman

The fire service is open to men and women over 18. Some fire brigades take on 16- and 17-year-olds. They are given basic training. At 18 they can be fully operational. Firefighters, besides fighting fires, are called to all sorts of accidents. They may also visit homes, factories and schools to demonstrate fire prevention. Like many jobs, firefighting has its own jargon. The exercises here will help you to understand this jargon. We can also pick up useful knowledge about fire prevention.

*Read the **Words you need**. Study the special jargon and the information on fire prevention. Then see if you can answer all the questions.

Words you need

flammable or **inflammable** easily catches fire
corrosive rusting or eating away
radio-active giving off rays that can penetrate matter

spontaneously combustible able to catch fire by heat generated within the substance itself

Special jargon

Below Look out below. Shouted by firefighters when coming down the pole.
Train Rotate, turn round (used of a ladder).
Knock off Finish; stop pumping.
Make up Put things away.
Under run Empty hoses.
Stand from under Tells people below that something is being dropped from above.

Fire prevention

Many fires are caused by carelessness. Here are some things to look out for.

Electrical flex under carpets or lino can get worn, yet go unnoticed.

Have chimneys swept regularly.

Appliances wired to one socket can overload the circuit.

Flex or cable joints: use proper connectors.

Switch off TV and other electrical appliances when not in use. Pull out electric plugs.

A mirror over the fireplace encourages people to get too near the fire.

Keep a fire hearth clean.

? Questions

1 What does a fireman shout when coming down the pole?

2 A firewoman is on top of a building. She drops some damaged material to the ground. What should she shout?

3 Name one liquid which carries this sign on its container:

4 A tanker carrying acids has a special sign. Draw it here:

5 Look at the picture below. There are eleven danger points. Each one could be the cause of a fire. Can you say what each of the danger points is?

a _____
b _____
c _____
d _____
e _____
f _____
g _____
h _____
i _____
j _____
k _____

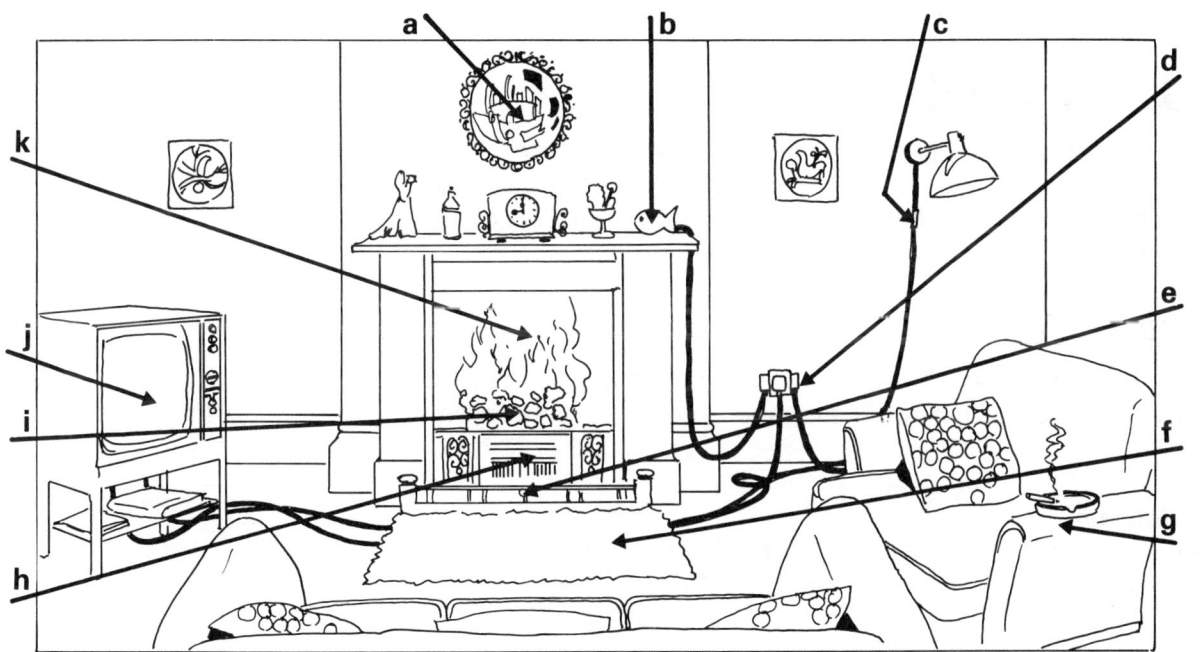

6 Can you name some of the qualities that firefighters need?

7 Why do you think it is sometimes better to use signs rather than words?

113

Armed services

You want to enlist in the armed services? Then you will have to pass certain medical and aptitude tests. If you are over 17 and suitable, you may choose from over 150 trades and skills. Some, however, are only available to people on long contracts. In the case of the army you can apply whilst still at school. Then you can take up your place between 16 and 17½ as an army junior. Your further education is important in the armed services. You will be encouraged to attend courses and gain qualifications.

The armed services also have a Youth Training Scheme (ASYS). This is a two year course. You may leave it provided you give 14 days notice in writing. An allowance of £26.25 per week is made. The cost of food and accommodation is deducted from this. You receive the same basic training as a regular soldier and some will go on to learn skills and trades.

The exercises here are concerned with some activities of army recruits. There is as much variety in the armed services as in civilian life. For further information find the appropriate branch in Yellow Pages. Your careers officer will also help.

*Read the **Words you need**. Study the information on junior soldiers. Then answer the questions.

Words you need

civilian person not in the services
civvy street civilian life
eligible fit for the job; suitable to be chosen

ONC Ordinary National Certificate
potential ability for the future
recruit new soldier

? Questions

To get essential meaning from a text we must: **a** think about what we are reading; **b** ask questions; **c** put these questions in order of priority; **d** be able to sum up the main points.

Junior Soldiers

We know that not everyone is interested in passing exams or getting involved in a technical career.

Perhaps you'd agree with this thought.

Then what might suit you down to the ground is a place as a Junior Soldier.

But we'll have to make no bones about it.

You have to be the tough, outdoor type ready to take anything in your stride.

And the more you put into it, the more you get out of it.

In the Infantry for example you'll be handling anti-tank guns, mortars and machine guns.

You could also learn to drive and operate radios.

If we find you're the responsible type, you're in line for early promotion after your basic training.

By the time you're 17½ you'll be a fully trained soldier ready to take your place in the arm or corps of your choice.

Most courses last about a year, but sometimes an extra term of four months is needed to pack in all the training.

---

1 Who is eligible?
2 What sorts of things would you handle?
3 What can it lead to?

1 Look at the passage on Junior Soldiers. The three questions have been asked for you. Do the same for 'Apprentices'.

Apprentices

To make the grade as an Army Apprentice is by no means easy, but it's worth it.

The Apprentices Colleges are some of the finest training establishments in the country.

And very much the envy of civilian firms.

The teaching staff are real experts. They can teach you a trade in half the time it takes in civvy street.

And you don't need 'O' levels.

Just a natural talent and the ability to make the most of the expert training.

For some trades, the training lasts for two to three years but at the end you'll be able to take your place as one of the most technical men in the Professionals.

You'll be ready for promotion and you'll have earned some qualifications on the way.

Besides your ONC or City and Guilds, you could easily have picked up a few 'O' levels, even 'A' levels, on the way.

The trades you choose vary from electronics to bricklaying, but whatever you specialise in makes you a very valuable man to the Army.

Your three questions

1 _____
2 _____
3 _____

Summary (fill in the missing words)

You are taught by experts in _____ Colleges. You don't need written _____ just _____ and ability. The technical _____ for some trades lasts for 2–3 years. Then, with some qualifications you'll be ready for _____. Whatever trade you choose, you'll become very _____ to the army.

Junior Leader

If you are tough, fit, like sports and outdoor life, with average ability at school subjects, this could be the life for you.

It's an active, busy life as a Junior Leader because you go where the action is.

You'll learn to handle responsibility, take decisions, be a leader because today's Junior Leaders are tomorrow's Army NCOs.

Training courses last about a year, some slightly longer.

In that time you'll pack in all the adventure training and new pastimes you can handle.

You'll probably get abroad too.

If you have the potential to pass your 'O' levels and CSE exams we have the facilities to assist you in obtaining these certificates together with the offer of further education.

Your further education is important to us, because we want you to climb as high up the ladder as you can get.

Your three questions

1 _____
_____
2 _____
_____
3 _____
_____

Summary

_____
_____
_____
_____
_____
_____
_____
_____
_____
_____

Community Service Volunteers (CSV)

CSV is a national volunteer agency. It aims to involve people in *community* work and encourage social change. CSV's main concern is with young people. By their involvement they should learn to help the community. They will also develop their own *potential*. CSV never rejects any *volunteer*. Everyone over 16 is accepted. In this section we give some information on CSV to demonstrate the opportunities that CSV offers. This will also help in the development of reading/writing skills.

*Read the **Words you need** carefully. Do you know them? Then read the information passages and answer the questions.

Words you need

community the public in general
discretionary according to the decision of the authority
reviewed annually assessed each year

voluntary willingly; done by free choice
volunteer one who enters service freely

CSV is a national organisation which, amongst other things, involves young people in full-time voluntary work. It involves caring for others and working for change in society. All over Britain, CSV is at work with the physically and mentally handicapped. They work with young people who need special care. They work with the elderly and the homeless. In fact, they work wherever the need is greatest.

You could become a volunteer. If you can commit yourself, CSV think you have a right to do so. Everyone has something to offer. All volunteers under 35 and able to involve themselves full-time are placed in projects. No one is rejected.

Experience is not required. Most of all CSV welcomes freshness and imagination. If you are good at sports or crafts, have hobbies, can make people laugh, CSV would like to hear from you. If you've done a course, they will use your skills.

How long will I be a Community Service Volunteer?
We'd like you to work for a year, but you can commit yourself for as little as four months.

How about money?
Your project will provide you with pocket money (currently £13 a week), all meals (or a weekly food allowance of up to £15.50) and, if you are placed in a project away from home, rent free accommodation. You will also receive your return fare from your home to the project at the beginning and end of your placement, plus any fares or other out-of-pocket expenses you might incur while working there as a volunteer.

After every four months as a CSV, you are entitled to one week's paid holiday away from the project and your return fare home. A discretionary personal clothing allowance may be available after your first four months.

CSVs do not need to pay tax or national insurance.

? Questions

1 You don't get paid on CSV work. However, you do get pocket money. How much? _____

2 You also get all meals free or an allowance for food. How much is the allowance? _____

3 When do you become entitled to one week's holiday and return fare home? _____

4 What else may become available to you at this time? _____

5 Look at the information on CSV on page 116. The first paragraph tells us about CSV. Can you think of a title for this paragraph which is also a question?
What _____?

6 Most paragraphs start with the main idea. They then give you more detail. What are the important details of paragraph 1?
_____
_____

7 Look at the second paragraph. Give a title for this paragraph. What is the main idea? What are the essential details?
Title _____ Main idea _____
Details _____

8 Look at the third paragraph. Give it a title. State the main idea. Write down the essential details.
Title _____ Main idea _____
Details _____

9 If you decided to become a volunteer, what work would you like? Why?
_____

Revision

1 Do you know the meaning of these words? Write their meaning on the lines provided.

a Aptitude _____

b Deducted _____

c Illegal _____

d Incident _____

e Inflammable _____

f Community _____

2 Think of some other public service jobs. Write on the lines provided the ones you could apply for:

_____

_____

_____

_____

_____

_____

3 On page 109 we did a 'same or opposite' test. Find the two words on each line which are the same or opposite. Write the letters of those words at the end of the lines.

Answer

1 SAME   A enlist B army C air force D enrol   ___ ___

2 OPPOSITE   A criminal B legal C detective D illegal   ___ ___

3 SAME   A soldier B voluntary C willing D civilian   ___ ___

4 OPPOSITE   A careful B helpful C plentiful D careless   ___ ___

5 OPPOSITE   A uniform B military C civilian D police   ___ ___

4 Accuracy in checking. Look at the names and addresses in column A. Now check the names and addresses which have been copied into column B. Where you find a mistake, draw a ring round it.

A	B
Mr G Stringer The Serpentine, Crosby	Mr G Stringer The Serpentine, Crowley
Mrs A Mockler 2 Argos Place, Brighton	Mrs A Mockler 2 Argos Place, Brighton
Mr Arthur Bennett 524 Kingsway, Chester	Mr Albert Bennett 524 Kingsway, Chester
Miss Jackie Tiffin 301 Hereford Drive, Poole	Miss Jackie Tiffin 301 Hereford Drive, Poule

5 Read the section from a fire brigade guide below. Then answer the questions.

a What is the subject of the guide?

b What is the main idea of the second paragraph?

c If you are caught in smoke, what should you do?

d What is the main idea of the last paragraph?

- When fire breaks out, how can you escape? This guide will give you directions on how to escape from houses or high-rise buildings during a fire.

- Smoke can choke and kill you after a few breaths. It is your worst enemy. If you are caught in smoke, get down onto the floor and crawl.

- The lift is another enemy. It can trap you. If the lift's signals are triggered by heat, it can get stuck on the floor where the fire is. You wouldn't want to be trapped inside. Always look to see where the exit stairs are. Use them to get below the floor where the fire is and to get out of the building.

6 Which of these titles is best suited to the passage above?
a 'Smoke Can Choke'
b 'Trapped in a Lift'
c 'Escaping from a Fire'.

7 On the lines below, write the essential details of the final paragraph in this passage.

8 Look at the picture below. It is an interview. Apart from name, address and age, what will the interviewer want to know? Make a list here:

9 Read the following facts. Then use the five *W*s and one *H* to help you fill out the written report.

Suppose that you're a police officer on patrol on 30 March at 10.30 p.m. You see a man lying on the footpath at the southern corner of Albert Avenue and Park Parade. He tells you that he has just been hit on the head by a man he describes as wearing a black jumper. He says that his attacker also robbed him of his watch and wallet containing £150 in cash, his driving licence and two credit cards. The victim gives his name as John Miller of 23 Wattle Street. You take him to the hospital, where he is found to have bruises on his head and right arm. Later, you are again on patrol near the scene of the incident. You see a man in a dark jumper hiding in a doorway. You decide that he is a suspect and that he should come with you to the police station for questioning. His name is Bill White and his address is 267 Waterworks Street. He has £150 in his pocket.

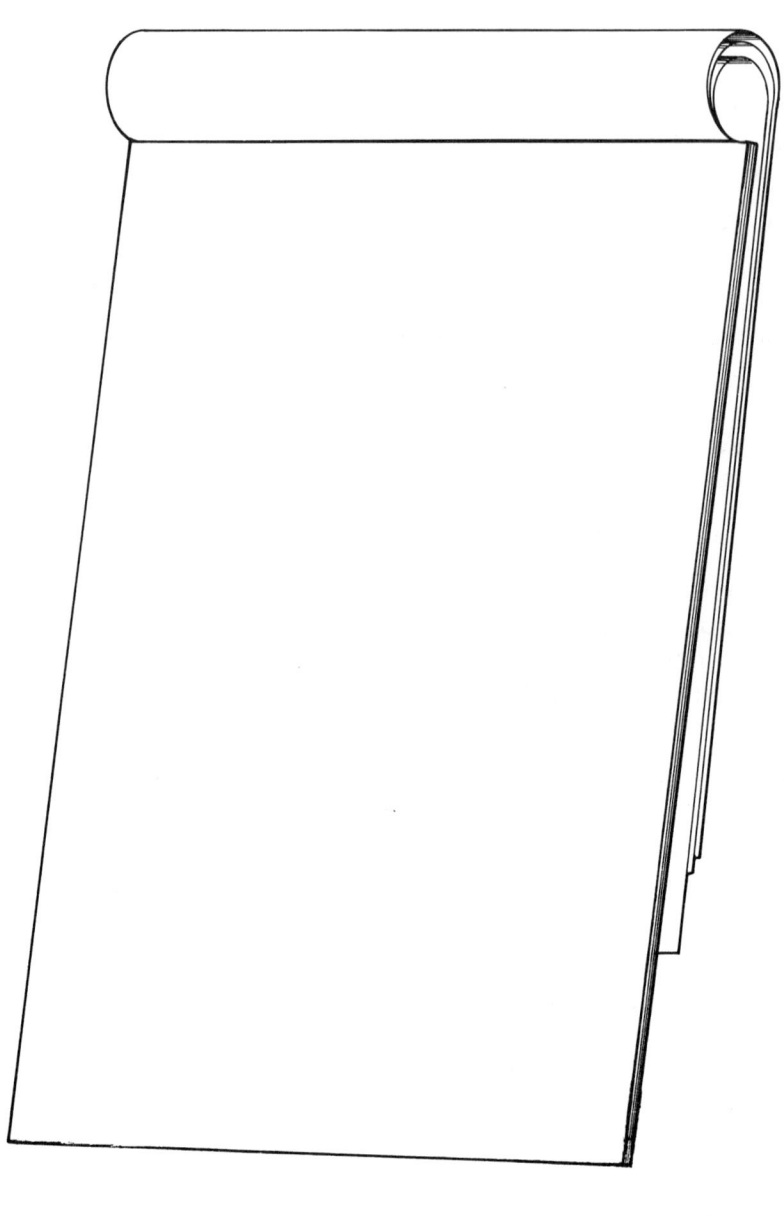

10 What evidence would be required to prove that Bill White is guilty? Make a note here of the evidence you have and the evidence you require:

_____
_____
_____
_____

More about the jobs in this book

This book does not give a complete picture of the selected jobs and schemes. It does provide some of the reading and writing skills involved in them. Further information on these jobs can be found in the school careers library. Next to each job we have listed the letters which refer to it. For instance, next to 'Plumber' you will see the letters 'UF'. If you need information on plumbing, look up 'UF' in the school careers library.

Unit 3: Office jobs

Job	Reference	Additional Information
Clerk	CAV	
Receptionist/telephonist	CAV	
Office machine operator	CAV	
Typist	CAV	
Secretary	CAT; CAP	

Unit 4: Social jobs

Job	Reference	Additional Information
Shop assistant	OF	Look under Retail Trade
Dry-cleaning shop assistant	OF	Look under Retail Trade. See also IG – Dry-cleaning
Waiter/waitress	IC	Hotel work
Nurse (E.N.(G))	JAD	Look under Nursing
Cashier (in a shop)	OFA	

Unit 5: Practical jobs

Job	Reference	Additional Information
Assembly worker	S; R	Assembly work
Carpenter	UF	See also Cabinet Making (SAJ)
Plumbing	UF	Plumbing
Electrician	RAK	
Motor mechanic	RAE	See also Vehicle Body Repair (RON)

Unit 6: Active/outdoor jobs

Job	Reference	Additional Information
Forecourt sales staff	OFL	Commonly known as Service Station Staff
Delivery person	YAD	
Building worker	UF	
Glazier	UF	
General farm worker	WAB	

Unit 7: Artistic jobs

Job	Reference	Additional Information
Hairdresser	IL	Hairdressing
Florist's assistant	OFM	Floristry. See also Horticulture (WAD)
Photographer	EV	See also Journalism (FAC) and Medical Photography (JOG)
Dressmaker	SAH	
Signwriter	ET	

Unit 8: Public service jobs

Job	Reference	Additional Information
Postman/woman	YAT	See also Post Office Administration (CAM)
Police officer	MAB	
Fireman/firewoman	MAF	
Armed services	B	See also Army – Other Ranks (BAG)
Community Service Volunteers	EG	

Personal notes

This page could be useful for quick reference when out of regular employment or when seeking work.

About you

Surname _____ First names _____ Date of birth _____

Address _____ Postcode _____

Name and address of last school _____ Telephone _____

Any qualifications (include courses and experience) Date passed

_____ _____
_____ _____
_____ _____
_____ _____

National Insurance Number: _____

Two referees (people who will give you a reference)

Names	Addresses	Telephone

Careers Officer

Name	Address	Telephone

UBO	Office address	Telephone

DHSS	Address (office)	Telephone